More Praise for
THE ALTERNATIVE ANSWER

"*The Alternative Answer* is a must-read for investors and advisors! Bob demystifies the world of alternative investments, and offers his unique perspective on how to use and evaluate the various types of strategies and structures. **The Alternative Answer is destined to become an instant classic.**"
—Tony Davidow, alternative beta and asset allocation strategist, Schwab Center for Financial Research

"This is no pie-in-the-sky guide to unearthing the next can't-miss penny stock or the next pathbreaking technology too secret to be named. **Rice offers sophisticated, easily accessible advice for using alternative investments to build a portfolio that's likely to generate solid gains in an age of anemic returns, yet still be resilient enough to weather a global financial crisis.**"
—Peter Passell, senior fellow, the Milken Institute, and author of *Where to Put Your Money Now*

"Stocks have gone nowhere for thirteen years and bonds offer no yield. Investors sense there must be good alternatives, but don't know where to look. Help is on the way! Bob Rice has written a timely and invaluable guide to the world of alternative investing. *The Alternative Answer* presents a clear path through the minefield of alternatives so that you can arrive safely in the promised land of higher returns without undue risk. This book is your first step on the road to increased income, wealth preservation, and a more secure retirement."

—James Rickards, author of the national bestseller
Currency Wars: The Making of the Next Global Crisis

"Rice has provided a great service and a timely educational tool for the most overlooked and underserved class of investors: average Americans. This book needed to be written and Rice's timing is perfect."

—Guy Haselmann, director, U.S. Rate Sales
and Strategy, Scotiabank

"Bob Rice has written the ultimate primer on alternative investments, a necessary component of any investment strategy, regardless of sophistication or net worth."

—Stephen L. Weiss, managing partner,
Short Hills Capital Partners, LLC and
author of *Unhinged* and *The Big Win*

"Bob Rice takes a crowbar and pries open the door to alternative investments. With clear prose and wise counsel, he reveals the formerly off-limits world of hedge funds, futures, and partnerships."

—Todd G. Buchholz, former managing director of the Tiger
hedge fund and author of *Rush: Why We Thrive in the Rat Race*

THE
ALTERNATIVE
ANSWER

THE
ALTERNATIVE
ANSWER

The Nontraditional Investments
That Drive the World's
Best-Performing Portfolios

BOB RICE

HARPER
BUSINESS

An Imprint of HarperCollins*Publishers*
www.harpercollins.com

HarperCollins books may be purchased for educational, business, or sales promotional use. For information, please e-mail the Special Markets Department at SPsales@harpercollins.com.

FIRST EDITION

Designed by William Ruoto

Library of Congress Cataloging-in-Publication Data
    Rice, Bob.
    The alternative answer : the nontraditional investments that drive the world's best-performing portfolios / Bob Rice.—First edition.
        p.   cm
    ISBN 978-0-06-225790-1
    1. Portfolio management. 2. Investments. 3. Finance, Personal. I. Title.
HG4529.5.R53   2013
332.63—dc23   2013003931

13 14 15 16 17   OV/RRD   10 9 8 7 6 5 4 3

Contents

Introduction

We've been taught that the investing universe is made up of stocks, bonds, and maybe some real estate. But elite investors know those categories represent only a fraction of the real possibilities . . . and that by broadening their choices they can, and do, dramatically improve their total returns while simultaneously reducing their risks of big losses. That the rest of us didn't even know about these "alternative investments" hardly mattered, because we couldn't invest in them anyway. That has changed. Today nearly all investors should be expanding their investment horizons to profit from these new opportunities . . . and also to protect themselves from the inevitable next major market shock. That's what this book is about.

Admittedly, the vocabulary of this world is a bit odd, but the ideas are not difficult. Over my thirty-year tour of duty in alternatives—as a lawyer, investor, entrepreneur, and director of broker-dealer and asset management firms—I've constantly been amused by the way these relatively straightforward concepts are wrapped in such crazy lingo. After all, the original "alternative investors" were the European aristocracy who threw their art and gold into saddlebags, fled temporarily, and later returned to their timberlands. And somehow they managed all that without ever hearing a peep about reversion to the mean.

Even the original hedge fund manager—Benjamin Graham, the hero of Warren Buffett, in fact—was just a classic value investor who recognized that simply buying cheap stocks while simultaneously shorting expensive ones would create profits regardless of overall market movement. If you've never had anyone explain to you exactly how "long/short" strategies work (you're about to), it may seem marvelous and sound oxymoronic; but once you have, it's pedestrian.

And so it goes. The language and tactics may be unfamiliar, but the core ideas are vital. The "secrets" of alternatives, so effectively used by the world's top investors for decades, are essential tools for anyone hoping to survive financially when more common options are volatile, limited, and unrewarding.

Now, obviously, everyone approaches this topic with different financial needs and goals. Therefore, to make the book as useful as possible, it's organized around the four essential jobs that investments can perform:

> **Job 1**: Generate greater income than typical fixed income instruments provide, with a focus on income that rises with inflation.
>
> **Job 2**: Reduce overall risk by diversifying into a radically broader set of strategies and assets, and by incorporating insurance against stock downturns.
>
> **Job 3**: Enhance long-term growth through opportunities with substantially more upside than traditional investments.
>
> **Job 4**: Protect purchasing power from inflation, currency devaluation, and crises.

As we progress you'll discover dozens of new strategies and asset classes, from royalty rights to global macro funds, and from start-up investing to timber. Certainly not every option will be suitable for all investors, but there is one common, ultimate goal: to maximize returns *and* mitigate risks.

If you already know a bit about alternatives, you may be surprised to see that the content is not organized by subjects like "Private Equity" or "Real Assets" or "Hedge Funds." Rest assured, they're explained in full. But these labels are of little practical use to investors, not only because of extensive real-world overlap, but now also because the picture has been blurred by new mutual funds and **ETFs**[*] that deploy many of the same strategies.

Instead, we'll start with an overall explanation of why and how alternative strategies work (chapters 2 and 3), describe the vehicles in which you'll find them (chapter 4), and then go in to more strategy-specific detail as we describe how investors of different financial status can fill those four jobs (chapters 5 to 8).

The entire story is brought together in "The Big Picture," chapter 9, with model portfolios tuned to different levels of wealth and liquidity, and also to the investor's view of our long-term economic prospects (you'll hear mine). Then you'll get all the tools necessary to get to work, with a list of resources for help in finding opportunities, the key questions to ask before investing, and a glossary.

OK. If you're new to the subject, you might want to just pop right over to chapter 1 and dive in. Have fun! If you are already familiar with the topic, an investment professional, or just really curious about the book's conceptual framework, stick around for a few more paragraphs.

Perhaps you're wondering how the contents relate to what you already know about the alternatives landscape. So, for your convenience (meaning, so you can decide whether you actually want to read the book or not!), here's a summary.

---

[*] Definitions of boldfaced terms may be found in the glossary.

The basic approach is an adaptation of the strategic asset allocation model that endowments have used for years, one that reflects two critical modifications. First, there's great focus on liquidity and inflation-protected income. Second, it incorporates the latest analysis regarding portfolio construction, specifically regarding accumulation of risk premiums and avoidance of cross-asset class vulnerabilities. You might say the result is something of a "postendowment" model.

Many of the terms used in the book will be familiar, but they're used in a particular way and in a particular hierarchy. So here's a digest.

The conceptual starting point is that portfolios should be "panoramic" and "risk-tolerant." Panoramic portfolios are highly diverse, taking advantage of all available assets classes and strategies for income and growth across broad-time horizons. One underlying theme is that, despite the obvious importance of liquidity, many high-net-worth investors and family offices are overlooking excellent long-term opportunities given the high illiquidity premiums the market is offering.

The coequal principle is that the portfolio must be risk-tolerant. This has three aspects. First, most liquid securities should be held in strategies involving active risk management to protect against loss.

Second, portfolios should house assets and strategies that produce "uncorrelated" returns, responding independently to different kinds of economic environments. One test of a risk-tolerant portfolio is whether it includes both "convergent" and "divergent" strategies. As creatures of modern portfolio theory, convergent strategies tend to do well in normal markets; but divergent strategies are superior during periods of higher volatility, probably because they are based on the very different dynamics of supply/demand and behavioral economics.

Third, risk-tolerant portfolios should be "absolutely diversified," with a focus on *vulnerability* diversification. This goes beyond "noncorrelation" and even beyond the concepts of convergent and divergent strategies in ensuring that the various investments are not all subject to a given systemic risk (e.g., another credit freeze), economic regime (e.g., inflation or deflation), or geopolitical event.

Modern investors need modern tools. And they exist; it's just that there's been no reliable user's guide. Now, I hope, there is.

THE
ALTERNATIVE
ANSWER

CHAPTER 1

The Alternative Manifesto

Divide your portion to seven, or eight, for you do not know
what misfortune may occur on earth.
—KING SOLOMON, ECCLESIASTES 11:2

Yale's endowment is up 100% over the past, extraordinarily difficult, decade. I won't ask how you did.

So, what's up? Using all that IQ to pick great stocks? Hardly. The trick, in fact, is that mostly they aren't picking stocks at all: in 2012, only 6% of Yale's portfolio was in U.S. equities. Instead, fully half resided in things called "absolute return," "private equity," and "real assets" strategies. Another big chunk was in emerging markets. Those are the secret ingredients of an investing formula that is now widely followed by most other endowments, foundations, and the rest of the smartest money on the planet.

The lesson is loud: in our ever more volatile and complex world, a long-only, domestic stock and bond portfolio is inadequate. Those traditional securities represent only a tiny sliver of the potential investment universe: many of the best opportunities are, simply, elsewhere. Even more to the point, the biggest key to long-term wealth is loss avoidance; and, as I bet you've noticed, traditional portfolios are subject to periodic, devastating, crashes.

Until very recently, there wasn't much typical investors could do to expand their horizons or limit their downsides. Not to diminish their spectacular results, but those institutional investors and their ultrawealthy friends have had an unfair advantage: access to strategies and vehicles that were both unknown and unavailable to the rest of us.

That is changing extremely rapidly. Average investors are no longer stuck with the children's menu of investment options.

But what about the standard investing gospel, like our much-beloved 60/40 stock-bond portfolio? Are the old rules really passé? Well, in the most recent (and certainly not last) crisis, they provided about as much protection as a five-dollar umbrella in a hurricane, but you knew that. The real issue is that our bedrock principles actually have quite a poor long-term track record for safety and consistent returns. Let's consider the three big rules that everyone's been taught . . . but that are wrong.

Mistake 1: A 60% Stock/40% Bond Portfolio Is Ideal. At first glance, the results of this standard allocation don't look so horrible: a long-term average annual return of 4%. But this is a wonderful example of just how misleading statistics can be. The damning truth is such a portfolio suffered six collapses in the last century in which the losses exceeded 20% . . . utter disasters that each took more than a decade to recover from in real terms. There is no reason to expect this pattern to change.

Another way to look at that long-term average: throw a dart at a list of the last hundred years, and pretend you had invested in whatever year it hits. The odds are nearly 25% that, a full decade later, such a position would have shown a loss. That sound like a conservative strategy to you?

OK, but those bad periods aside, surely the rest of the time the returns have been great? Hardly. We've had eleven decades of experience with annually rebalanced 60/40 portfolios since 1900.

In the majority of cases, seven out of those eleven, the average annual real return was *less than 1%*. Surprisingly, the current Mojave Desert of returns is absolutely historically normal.*

That gaudy 4% average annual return is explained by just four absolutely exceptional decades: the '20s and '50s (postwar periods), and the '80s and '90s (the end of yet another war, this time cold; and our unrepeatable debt accumulation, which we're now working off). So unless you think we're on the cusp of another historically anomalous growth period, 60/40 is not the way to go. At least, not without a camel.

Even that history doesn't relate the whole scary story. The bond bubble that's been expanding for decades makes the "safe" component of a 60/40 portfolio into a potential hand grenade. The last period in which Treasury bond valuations were comparable to today's was followed by forty-five years of negative real returns. Forgetting history, it's simple common sense that the Fed's ferociously loose monetary policy makes inflation, and a major tumble in bond prices, highly likely at some point. And, no, it won't work to simply hold the bonds to maturity so you get all your principal back, because those dollars will have, by definition, then lost major purchasing power. That's precisely what bonds are supposed to protect.

Mistake 2: Stock Diversification Equals Safety. The standard method of "diversification" involves spreading stock selections across the "nine buckets." Those are defined by a matrix with "small, medium, and large" down the side, and "growth, blend, and value" across the top. Fill up all the buckets, and you're good to go. But, as you know, the crash emptied all nine at once.

---

* Bradly A. Jones, Deutsche Bank AG, "Rethinking Portfolio Construction and Risk Management," January 2012 white paper.

Well, maybe we should have included foreign equities, too? Not a terrible idea, certainly, but that won't get you the sort of diversification that yields safety. That idea may have helped when world markets sang in different keys; today, however, they have fulfilled the ardent wishes of that famous old Coke commercial, and learned to sing in perfect harmony.

Well, then, what about diversification across asset classes? That's headed in the right direction, but is still not enough; my guess is that in the Great Recession your home value didn't exactly cushion your stock losses. Merely spreading dollars around, even among apparently many different assets or strategies, does not necessarily provide the safety we need. A key reason is that some assets are inherently more volatile than others, so that dollar weighting does not equal risk weighting. For example, the long-term performance of a 60/40 stock/bond portfolio mimics a stock-only portfolio nearly perfectly: 95% of the combined volatility is driven by stocks alone. Bonds do almost nothing to balance out stock performance.

The crash was so devastating for a different reason, though. It turns out that apparently diverse asset categories can share an unnoticed Achilles' heel (often, leverage). Forgive the trite example, but different financial assets can be taken out by a single risk in much the same way that different telecommunications systems—phone, television, and the Internet—all bit the dust in Hurricane Sandy for "triple play" customers who relied on a single wire for all three.

The way to address this sort of risk is by emphasizing "uncorrelated" income streams and "absolute diversification" in the portfolio. We'll dive into this later, but meantime here's an interesting fact to hold you over: the biggest timberland owner in New Zealand happens to be . . . Harvard. Now, we're not exactly suggesting that you start buying trees on the other side of the planet (yet), but good modern investors will certainly adopt radically broader portfolios in aiming for safety.

Mistake 3: Buy and Hold [insert asset class here] Always Wins in the Long Run. No parent trying to pay tuition from a devastated college fund needs to hear what's wrong with this idea. Nor do folks who once thought real estate "can't go down, because they aren't making any more of it" . . . as this is written, fully one-fifth of all U.S. homes remain substantially less valuable than the mortgage on them. Maybe the Fed's desperate attempts to engineer inflation to fix this problem will eventually work, but those homeowners will never recover what they toss away each month on the underwater mortgage.

Stubbornly holding on to assets as they head south can just kill you. The cruel math of losses means that a 50% loss—from $100 to $50—requires a 100% gain—from $50 to $100—to break even. It's simply unrealistic to expect people with periodic (and often unpredictable) actual cash needs to wait through these cycles long enough to recover.

Instead, investors should be looking at portfolios with internal shock absorbers that are designed to minimize losses in the first place, or even profit in periods of general turmoil. There are an array of new options for this: you can turn to simple solutions like basic long/short mutual funds, or go exotic with a "global macro" manager. Much more on all this later.

So how then, you might ask, did these traditional investing ideas become so ingrained as common wisdom? In retrospect, it's not really a huge surprise. America has happily experienced a long and absolutely unprecedented stretch of economic prosperity and political hegemony. The factors behind that are legion: a superior political system; an open culture; success in the big wars; favorable demographics and immigration waves that captured talent; a superior education system and strong work ethic; vast natural resources; and many other wondrous elements that combined into the greatest country, and the most prolonged economic miracle, the world has ever seen.

Naturally, that created an investment opportunity like no other. In fact, for a very long time, it was hard to be wrong, so long as you were long . . . anything. So, sure, 60/40 sort of worked, just as most other combinations did; waiting out dips made sense; and "diversification" among a bunch of similar boats, simultaneously floating ever higher, felt real.

But the world has gotten infinitely more . . . well, complicated. I'm an optimist, but still: with algorithms executing billions of trades in nanoseconds without the slightest chance of intervention by human judgment, markets will remain frighteningly unstable, or grow more so. The absurdly overleveraged Western governments will try to print their way out of their debts, which could lead to massive inflation if they succeed, or massive deflation if they fail. World economies have become one long domino chain. The technology and information revolution will continue to make us more efficient in every possible way . . . likely creating growing structural unemployment and income inequality. Toss in cyberterrorism, climate change, political gridlock, and military flareups, and the picture could take just a bit of the shine off your otherwise lovely day.

Simply put, it would be foolish to ignore these new and profound risks when investing. But it would be equally foolish to ignore the enormous and plentiful new opportunities inherent in our changing world. Just consider how many ways wealth will be created from robotics, the maturation of the Asian and African economies, or the surprising transformation of America into the world's largest oil (and natural gas) producer, as the International Energy Agency predicts will happen over the next decade.

Thus, smart portfolios today must be *panoramic* and *risk-tolerant*. That's the alternatives manifesto.

A "panoramic" portfolio reaches across a wide spectrum of assets, strategies, and time horizons to achieve higher current yields and more long-term growth. Royalties, start-ups, water, distressed securities, infrastructure, frontier markets, specialty finance, oil and gas partnerships, roll-ups, art, farmland, and scores of other categories provide compelling new opportunities to meet investor needs, from current income to generational wealth protection.

A "risk-tolerant" portfolio is like fault-tolerant building: it can absorb major shocks without collapsing. Such stability requires active risk management to guard against sudden stock market declines; "uncorrelated" positions that generate returns independent of one another in typical business cycles; and "absolute diversification" so that strategies do not share a single point of failure in a crisis.

Now, the big news is not so much that alternative investments can provide much smarter and safer ways to generate income, grow portfolios, protect wealth, and transfer it . . . that is an empirical fact, but it's been known for many years. Rather, the headline is that these strategies are now accessible by nearly everyone, thanks to a slew of changes in the legal and business environment, and, bluntly, a growing realization even by the big brokerage houses that the old ways of doing things just aren't working.

As a result, a tidal wave of new financial products is hitting the market to address our new reality, and at the same time, classic hedge and private equity funds are finding ways to offer their strategies to the merely affluent instead of just the super-rich. Now, investors can get hedged exposure to the stock market through "smart beta" mutual funds; earn inflation-protected income via traded master limited partnership interests; diversify into commodities through managed futures; play private equity through new registered funds; and protect against currency and inflation risk with real-asset ETFs. Simultaneously, online platforms are springing up to offer direct investments in start-ups, corporate buyouts, commercial real estate, hedge funds, and all manner of other deals.

This plethora of new options and opportunities is certainly welcome, but a bit overwhelming. The simple goal of this book is to put them into perspective and show how to use them.

So here's the plan. First, we're going to explain exactly how and why it is that "panoramic" and "risk-tolerant" portfolios generate superior long-term results. Then we'll do a quick review of the basics of hedge funds, private equity, venture capital, managed futures, and real assets . . . and how they translate into new, different structures that allow almost any investor into these previously very exclusive opportunities.

That's all fine, but exactly which alternatives should you consider? That depends on the jobs you need done inside your portfolio. There are four: generating higher, inflation-protected current income; "broadening the base" to reduce overall portfolio risk; enhancing long-term upside with some bigger return strategies; and ensuring your purchasing power against crises and currency devaluation. For each job, eight specific alternative strategies are suggested.

"The Big Picture," chapter 9, then brings everything together with model blueprints for investors of different liquidity and wealth levels, and a discussion of which investments should do best under the various economic "regimes" we may see in the coming years. And, following that, we'll detail exactly what to look for if you do go shopping for alternatives, and where you can find them.

Finally, there's a big fat glossary. After digesting that, you'll be fully fluent.

Ready? Let's go.

CHAPTER 2

....

Do Alternatives Work?

I thank my fortune for it,
My ventures are not in one vessel trusted,
Nor to one place; nor is my whole estate
Upon the fortune of this present year.
—Antonio, *The Merchant of Venice*, Act I, Scene i

Most people think investing *means* stocks and bonds. We've been indoctrinated that way. After all, no news broadcast since childhood has been complete without a recap and explanation of Mr. Dow Jones's day, as normal as hearing about our family's trials and tribulations over dinner. He's one of us.

Well, yes he is. But just one. Other asset classes, like private equity and venture capital, have dramatically outperformed stocks for many years now (of course, it wasn't actually all that hard, but still . . .). Both of them dusted Mr. Jones by several percent over the past five years, and the edge really mounts up over time: PE more than doubled stock returns over the past ten years, while venture capital returns crushed them by more than 5x over the past fifteen.* At the same time, royalties and real assets provide, respectively, higher income and better inflation protection than traditional

---

* Cambridge Associates LLC U.S. Private Equity and Venture Capital Indexes, respectively.

securities. A panoramic portfolio, now within reach for typical investors, is really just common sense.

But in any family there are some members about whom people whisper. So in the interest of having a nice pleasant evening together, let's just clear the air about the most misunderstood of the alternative siblings. The ugly talk is fueled by this breaking news:

"Last quarter, the S&P outperformed the average hedge fund by 2%." The handsome anchor, with a knowing smile, manages to convey the folly of investing in something that didn't "even" beat the S&P. And many pretty knowledgeable viewers gently nod in agreement.

The most important lesson you can take away from this book is understanding what's wrong with that apparently innocuous headline.

Risk-Tolerant Investing

First off, on that same logic, our anchor might as well start his local sports report with this: "Area high school baseball, football, and basketball teams were all in action tonight, and their average score was thirty-four." *Hedge funds are not an asset class.* They encompass dozens of different kinds of strategies, all with very different risk-reward characteristics. Some do swing for the fences, maybe using a global macro style, while others patiently stamp out small, steady gains, perhaps in a convertible arbitrage strategy. We'll review the whole zoo later, but meanwhile: that "average" hedge fund would indeed be quite a sight, an investment platypus.

But we have to admit that all hedged strategies do share one common feature: active risk management. It's a universal feature of the species, like hair to a mammal. They are designed to buffer losses, and routinely dedicate a portion of their assets to downside protection.

Conversely, traditional "long only" investing is truly like driving a car without brakes: just fine going up a big hill, not so great on the other side. Hedged strategies do have brakes—and must pay for them by forgoing some gains in some markets. Since the "average hedge fund performance" number reflects that fact, it will often "underperform" the S&P when stocks are zooming up that hill. *But it's what happens coming down that matters most to your wealth in the long term.*

Thus, if we're going to talk about "average hedge fund performance," the most salient point to make is this: that platypus has dramatically outperformed stocks in every single one of the eleven big market downturns since 1987.

And that is why, *over time*, these strategies *do* outperform the stock market.

Here's the proof:

HEDGE FUND RETURNS COMPARED TO STOCK RETURNS

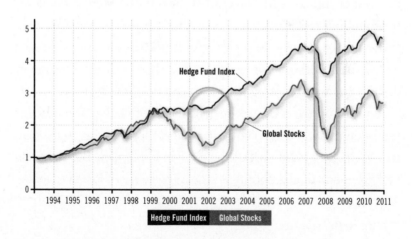

Source: Centre for Hedge Fund Research

Please note how clearly you can see that, indeed, the main reason our mythical average hedge fund has outperformed stocks is simple: *it didn't lose nearly as much in down periods.*

Don't forget: when you lose 50% in the market, you've got to score a 100% gain to get back to even. Clawing your way back is possible, but the long-term damage is never really undone. A ten-year investment of $100,000 that is flat in the first year, and then compounds at 8% each year thereafter, generates $200,000. But if the same initial investment falls by half in the first year, and then compounding at the same 8% rate, the ten-year wait just gets you back to even. A lost decade.

Now ask yourself: would it have been worth a small insurance premium to avoid that first year loss? That's what active risk management provides . . . and, yes, Mr. TV Anchor, there is a cost to that.

So that is the profoundly misunderstood point about hedged investing. It's not some risky new invention aimed at shooting the lights out every quarter; quite the opposite. Indeed, as you'll see in the next chapter, the basic tactics of the industry were invented by the founding father of classic value investing, Benjamin Graham. It was he, the spirit-guide of Warren Buffett, who started the first hedge fund (although it wasn't called that until a media-savvy disciple began promoting the idea a couple of decades later).

For all the focus on risk management, of course, those hedge funds aren't just trying to not lose money; they're trying to make it, too. We'll get to that part of the story in a moment. But first, let's hear from one final authority on the importance of loss aversion.

The Origin of the Hedging Species

And she is: Mother Nature. Humans are built for risk aversion, and like every other outcome of evolution, that tells you something.

Consider whether you'd take this onetime bet. We'll flip a coin and if it's heads, you owe me $10,000; if it's tails, though, you'll win $12,000. What's your instinctive reaction?

It's obvious that this proposition has a "positive expectancy." As you no doubt realize, *on average*, a gambler would win $1,000 by taking the bet. Yet, in the real world, almost no one will accept it. Why that is mystified all manner of social scientists, economists, and psychologists for many decades, but the answer is now enshrined in something called "prospect theory." To get people to accept the wager, we'd have to offer them something more along the lines of a 2:1 proposition, or maybe better. That is, we'd need to offer a $20,000 or $25,000 payoff to offset that possible $10,000 loss.

It's how we're wired: *losses hurt more than gains please*, and, therefore, to be attractive, a bet must offer a *lot* more of the latter than the former. No doubt, that default programming has arisen for exactly the reason the chart on page 13 shows what it does: not losing what you already have is the key to prosperity. Sure, maybe we learned that with the spoils of the hunt, but our instincts are no accident and remain correct.

Nonetheless, they weren't designed for probability analysis in fast-paced financial markets. Ask yourself these two pairs of questions, adapted from the fabulous book *Thinking, Fast and Slow*, by Nobel Prize winner Daniel Kahneman:

Pair One: Which would you choose?
A. Get $9,000 for sure
OR
B. Take a 90% chance to win $10,000

Pair Two: Which would you choose?
A. Lose $9,000 for sure
OR
B. Take a 90% chance to lose $10,000

If you're like nearly everybody else, you'll choose the first option in the first question, and the second option in the second. You might even make those choices fully realizing that mathematically there's no difference between them. And yet, study after study verifies that people nearly universally select A in the first pair, and B in the second.

You know why by now. We like sure things, and will do just about anything to avoid losses. As a result, from a mathematical standpoint, we're too conservative when choosing between two different but positive possible outcomes, and too aggressive when facing two different but negative ones. And that, ironically, means that our well-intentioned wiring often leads to poor financial decisions in rapid-fire markets.

Thus: as stocks rise, our tendency is to grab sure things and sell too soon. As prices fall, our aversion to recognizing losses makes us hold on, hoping to get back to even. It's the "retail curse": divorce your winners, marry your losers.* And when real panic sets in and we do finally sell, we subsequently fail to get back in soon enough for fear of even further losses. For average investors, reentry points are almost always well above exit points.

---

* By the way, prospect theory also helps explain why the housing market is taking so long to clear . . . people just can't stomach the sense of loss that goes with selling underneath their purchase price. Faced with two negative outcomes—sell and recognize the loss, or continue making payments on an underwater mortgage—they keep writing those checks, hoping that eventually the market will rebound and they'll miraculously escape the loss.

This is a primary reason why individual market timing doesn't work, and why you cannot be your own "active risk manager" by moving in and out of stocks.

Instead, serve your very correct instincts by building portfolios with *built-in* protection. Then, you won't be forced to rely on emotional, knee-jerk reactions in market gyrations, knowing that you're already protected against loss. To prepared investors, a big market downdraft is a little like a ride in the Tower of Terror: gut wrenching still, but they don't actually try to get out of the car.

Active risk management—using hedging strategies—is thus one key leg of the risk-tolerant stool we want to build; the other two are noncorrelation and absolute diversification.

These ideas are extensions of a simpler view of diversification, those old nine buckets of stocks. That "diversification" held up OK during decades of rising economic standards, American hegemony, and general global stability but, of course, proved grossly inadequate in the last crash.

The shock of 2007–8 was especially profound because most everyone had nodded off to a very popular economic lullaby. The tune may not have been so great, but the logic was absolutely hypnotic. It went something like this: financial returns follow the same sort of mathematical rhythms as do almost all systems in nature. We can look back at these over time to see how an asset has performed . . . and since we're talking patterns, how it will in the future. So (trumpets for the big idea): if we blend the investments just so, we can get the peaks of some financial return waves to negate the troughs of others . . . the investment equivalent of noise-canceling headphones.

Wonderful on blackboards, not so great in practice. As simple as it sounds: patterns break. Accidents happen. That your kid has never fallen off his bike doesn't mean he never will. In the last crash, assets that had always performed differently surprised everyone by springing into a cancan worthy of the Rockettes. Moreover, just as many different kinds of crops are destroyed by one hailstorm, different buckets of assets—even those that typically behave differently from one another—can be vulnerable to a single kind of economic risk.

Those observations show we need to improve the old-style diversification model. First, we'll strive to add more sources of "uncorrelated" returns. The greater the number of different returns patterns that are used to create overall portfolio balance, the less that balance will be affected by one or two unexpected behaviors. Big marching bands sound OK even if a few musicians are on the wrong page.

A subtly different but important additional layer of protection comes from "absolute diversification." This means assembling strategies that not only are uncorrelated, but also do not share a common vulnerability to a single economic shock. To repeat the "triple play" analogy: telephone, TV, and Internet perform very different (uncorrelated) communications functions for you, but all fail together if your cable wire comes down. The goal of absolute diversification is to avoid a repeat of the way overall portfolios crashed in the crisis because both stocks and housing were so susceptible to a freeze in the credit markets.

The new menu of alternatives makes all that much easier than it has been, as you'll see. In the meantime, here's a fun experiment you can perform at your next cocktail party to show off the impressive power of real noncorrelation. Fill a large glass vase with jelly beans—a couple thousand work well (buying tip: there are about 400 jelly beans to the pound). As your guests come in, offer them a prize for guessing the total, but ensure they write down their guesses discreetly; it's important that no guest knows how the others are answering. After everyone's arrived, calculate the average, start clinking your glass, and announce the results.

No one will get it right. The high and low numbers will be ludicrously wrong, and identifying the contestants always brings a laugh. But here's the amazing thing: the average of all the guesses will be shockingly close to exactly correct . . . often within single digits, nearly always within a percentage point or so. Try it.

What's going on here? Because everyone's guess is genuinely independent of everyone else's, the individual mistakes cancel one another out. It is a pure example of the power of de-correlating errors. Note, however, that if the guests talk about the numbers and estimate together, the average gets thrown way off the mark—that amplifies the mistakes instead of canceling them.

In a similar way, when we combine *genuinely independent* assets into one portfolio, the "mistakes" tend to negate one another. But thinking that a given set of stocks will do that—regardless of their past histories—is a fantasy.

Panoramic Portfolios

Let's get back to making money, always more fun to discuss than not losing it. The idea of a panoramic portfolio is to accumulate a much broader set of assets and strategies that generate growth and income, and also to focus on harvesting those over different time horizons.

Take a look at Harvard's 2012 portfolio. It had exactly 12% invested in its long U.S. stock positions. Add in 4% for U.S. bonds, and the Crimson had 16% of its noncash portfolio in assets to which most people dedicate 100% of theirs.

That 84% difference is alternatives, of course. But take a deeper look at exactly which "alternatives" we're talking about. Of that 84%, 16% was in "absolute return" strategies, meaning hedge funds. Real assets, private equity, and non-U.S. investments made up other big chunks. This mix provides a combination of short-term income, long-term wealth protection, inflation hedges, and participation in growth industries and economies. That's panoramic.

HARVARD UNIVERSITY PORTFOLIO—2012

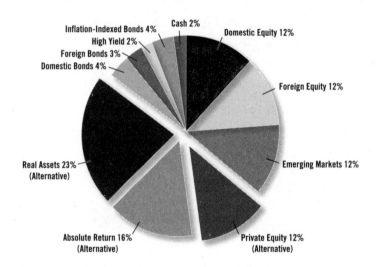

Source: Harvard University Endowment

The smart guys get it: stocks are just one asset class among dozens, not the single reference point from which everything else should be observed, referenced, and measured. Over any given short period, it simply doesn't matter whether this group of assets returns more or less than stocks alone do; over periods of years, this panoramic approach has handsomely outperformed them and, almost by necessity, will continue to do so over the next decades. How you can build your own version is the subject of the next several chapters.

For now, though, let's return to our anchorman, to whom I'd like to offer a bit of an apology. Yes, it's silly to talk about "average hedge funds," but he deserves credit for a deeper point, no matter how inelegantly it was stated. About one thing he was 100% correct: merely investing in hedged strategies certainly does not, by itself, generate automatically superior results.

On the one hand, you have the greats like Ray Dalio and Stanley Druckenmiller. Dalio runs Bridgewater, the world's largest hedge fund manager, and his "Pure Alpha" fund has generated over 16% per year for two decades, profiting along the way from the Mexican peso crisis, the Long Term Capital Management blowup, the tech bubble implosion, the crash of 2007–8, and the European sovereign wealth crisis. Druckenmiller's Duquesne Capital did even better, an incredible quarter-century run with average annual gains of 30% and not a single down year.

There aren't legions like these guys, but certainly there are hundreds of other managers who have assembled outstanding multiyear, market-beating track records with a savvy combination of risk management and opportunistic investing.

And then you have the bulk of the 9,000 or so hedge funds that now exist, up from maybe 500 when the industry became famous. (For perspective: there are only 5,000 publically traded stocks.) This is not Lake Wobegon, and those managers are not all above average. And surely the mere fact that they're pursuing some version of a hedged strategy does not automatically entitle them to outperformance.

This is a crucially important point, and it's true across the world of alternatives: *managers matter,* far more than they do in long-only strategies. The following graphic should make this clear. For eight investment approaches, four alternative and four traditional, it shows the difference between the best and worst managers. For each strategy, the taller the column, the greater that performance difference. The alternatives are grouped together to the left.

ANNUALIZED TEN-YEAR RETURN, 2002–2012

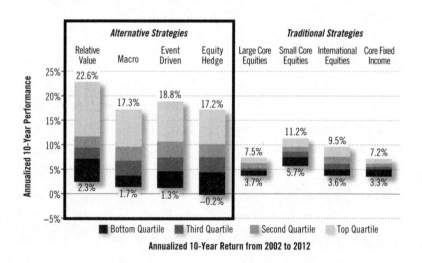

Source: Alpha Capital Management

There is a *hugely* wider performance gap between best and worst managers in the alternatives world (where the top ones generate ten or even fifteen times better returns than the laggards) than there is in the traditional investment world (where the difference is only about two times). Those disparities translate into wildly different gross returns in the alternatives world (22% versus 2% in the long/short category), but only modest ones with traditional managers (7.5% versus 3.7% for large-cap stocks).

And it's not just the top and bottom quartiles where these difference are pronounced; the performance ranges are much, much broader for the pretty good 25%, and the below-average 25%, too. This basic pattern also holds—and indeed is even more pronounced—among private equity, venture capital, and managed futures managers.

Why would that be true? Because stock pickers are playing a radically more standardized, restricted, and thoroughly explored game, with both many more rules and many fewer kinds of pieces, than are alternatives managers. In fact, the dominance of indexed investing nearly ensures reasonably uniform results for many stock strategies.

This is all a very big deal, and it's yet another reason why references to "average" hedge funds are so misleading. It may not be super unreasonable to refer to the average stock picker as representative of his class, because the performance disparity among the group is limited. But it's extremely unreasonable to refer to an average alternatives manager as representative of his class.

As you can guess, therefore, the competition to locate the best managers is even more intense in the alternatives world than it is among traditional investors. And that brings us to an unexpectedly tricky issue: how, exactly, to determine who really is good.

To start, let's ask this: if a drunk driver somehow gets home safely, was he smart to take the wheel?

You might instantly reject that as a stupid question, but investors routinely act as if the answer is yes. They judge the quality of investment decisions solely by results . . . profit is proof of prescience, and the biggest returns signal the best managers. It's a bit like judging the drunk's decision solely by whether he got home,

ignoring how much risk he took to get there . . . and then jumping
into the backseat for a ride the next time he leaves a party.

To demonstrate why it's difficult to tell lucky investment managers from good ones by just looking at gross returns, let's do an
experiment.

Say we start with 1,000 managers who are ideally mediocre:
each has a fifty-fifty chance of making or losing money over the
course of a year. After year one, we have 500 guys who profited.
Twelve months later, 250 have not had a down year. At the end
of year three, the magic number by the standards of Morningstar
and many other folks who report performance, we have 125 guys
who've made money every year and, by the way, outperformed
almost 90% of his peers.

At this point, these guys look like geniuses, and no doubt believe themselves to be. They'd be noticed by a young producer and
start popping up on TV, part of some "New Superstar Manager"
series. Another year goes by, and now 60 or so are now truly certi-
fied as gurus, having spent the year in the limelight while adding
to their unblemished records. Well, can you image what happens
to the 30 who then prosper yet again, picking stocks in between
keynote addresses and champagne toasts at Davos? At that point
these survivors probably all have many billions under management; heck, if they were running hedge funds, they might even be
closed to new investors and fabulously wealthy to boot.

(An excellent reason to start a hedge fund, by the way! You
have a 3% chance of pulling all this off, radically better than your
shot in the lotto, and you'll make much more money.)

Now imagine picking up the *Wall Street Journal* and reading a glowing article about one of those 3%. Without knowing
about the experiment, you'd feel great about investing with
him, wouldn't you? Who could possibly question a guy so fa-

mous, with a perfect five-year track record? Yet here, and in many real-world cases, the amazing record literally reflects pure dumb luck. And dumb luck reverses out, usually right after you invest.

So looking back at a few years of gross returns doesn't necessarily tell us whether a manager has been lucky or good. There are, however, ways to tell, famous statistical yardsticks like **Sharpe** and **Sortino** ratios. We'll describe these in detail later, but the headline is that both these measurements *divide a manager's performance by the risk he's taken to deliver it.*

Leaning further on the drunk driving analogy, these stats will show that some managers veered all over the road to get home, narrowly missing catastrophe, but that the good and sober ones stayed between the white lines all the way back.

Thus, the crucial question in evaluating money managers is what sort of *risk-adjusted* returns they produce over time. It's difficult for most investors to genuinely embrace that point. Higher gross returns sing an intoxicating siren song. But the law of averages always wins out in the long run, and managers with better risk-adjusted returns do, too.

And that brings us to the holy grail of the industry: **alpha**. This is the extra return a manager produces over a given index (say, the S&P) *to the extent he did not take additional risk to earn it.* Another way of saying the same thing is that alpha is generated by managers whose returns are higher, but not more volatile, than

---

* As measured by the volatility of those returns. In modern financial parlance, volatility and risk are the same thing. We're going to defer a detailed discussion of this until we learn a bit about modern portfolio theory in chapter 4. Meantime, if you just can't wait, see **Sortino ratio**, **Sharpe ratio**, **alpha**, **beta**, **R squared**, **sigma**, and **information ratio** in the glossary.

the overall market. It's not so easy to find alpha, but that's what the folks paying the classic "2 and 20" hedge fund fees are looking for.

There's also a more commonsensical way of thinking about alpha that works well for the broader investing universe in which this book operates. For our purposes, alpha is that unique value money managers generate for investors through skill and hard work, above the return that would be produced by an unmanaged investment in the same asset class. In the real world, nearly all managers who generate alpha are doing at least two things: working like demons and exploiting some specialized knowledge. That's true across all strategies and asset classes, from leveraged buyouts to art collecting.

So, for example, after a buyout, a private equity firm might reequip a car parts plant and retrain the workforce to increase margins, rather than just relying on leverage and a rising economy to make the investment pay off. A commodities trading advisor who's also a meteorologist might be among the first to grasp the likely severity of crop damage from a coming storm and hustle to put on the trades while profits can still be made. Successful venture capital firms nearly always contribute management and key relationships to their start-ups that improve the results. And, speaking of start-ups, entrepreneurs are the greatest alpha generators in our society.

This is an apt description of alpha even in the liquid stock markets to which the classic definition and all those ratios apply. Say a stock investor develops an information advantage by poring over the details in the footnotes of the financial statements of small, underfollowed stocks. He then has to not only decide whether and how that data is distilled into dominant market perceptions but also have the technical prowess, capital, discipline, and courage to trade the position correctly. Successful managers don't generate outsize returns just by coming up with some neat little trick for trading stocks that no one's ever thought of before . . . there are just way too many other geniuses with computers out there for that to work.

By the way, on that point, many academics hold to the idea that alpha isn't possible at all in publicly traded securities. I wonder how they would explain the profits made by one trader who, just over a decade ago, was sitting in his Midtown New York office drinking coffee and staring out his south-facing window. He stared at one of the most stunning sights in world history: an airliner flying into One World Trade. That this was no accident, as the earliest news reports had it, he understood immediately. Not until the second plane did most people realize what was going on. In between, he shorted the market through futures, yielding many millions that he later donated to charity.

The point is: data is one thing; meaning is something else. His superior understanding of a situation yielded an advantage. Note, however, that the advantage lasted only a few minutes and couldn't have been exploited by normal stock investors: the exchanges never opened that day. As in so many cases, the alpha was generated by speed and infrastructure as well as insight.

So that's one small but clear example of how and why professional managers can indeed outperform the market and generate alpha, even in the most liquid markets. Throughout the book, you'll encounter very many more.

In Review

Alternatives "work" because, over time, a portfolio of them delivers bigger and more diverse return streams, with fewer and smaller losses, than do standard investments. They are not designed to outperform stocks each and every quarter.

Private equity, venture capital, natural resources, foreign markets, and many hedged investing styles can provide much bigger returns than traditional stocks. Investors need "panoramic" portfolios to get ahead.

The biggest key to long-term wealth creation is loss avoidance. That requires a "risk-tolerant" portfolio that combines active risk management for liquid securities (hedged styles); a thorough mix of noncorrelated return streams; and investments that aren't all susceptible to a single type of economic risk.

Manager selection matters much more with alternatives than with stocks and bonds. Whereas the best stock pickers outperform the worst by 2x, the best alternative managers outperform the worst by 10x or more.

You can't tell how good a manger is by looking at gross returns, even over a few years; you must factor in how much risk they take. Risk-adjusted returns are the only reliable measure of performance.

Alpha, the "extra" performance that the very best managers deliver, is usually defined by mathematical formulas, but it can be more simply thought of as the result of skill and hard work.

Final Thought

Over time, the law of averages prevails. Investors who stick with managers, strategies, and portfolios with better *risk-adjusted* returns will end up richer. Sure, putting all your chips in the stock market is great when it's on a tear, but don't be fooled by short-term results. Math and history don't lie.

CHAPTER 3

....

Major Alternative Strategies

Science you don't know looks like magic.
—CHRISTOPHER MOORE

"Hedge funds" are a mystery. The mere phrase "private equity" helped cost Mitt Romney the presidency. "Real assets" do sound much better than fake ones, but, really, is that so special? And "managed futures" sound downright Orwellian.

Time for a little translation. After all, before deciding whether to buy into a strategy, we have to understand how it works. In the next chapter, we'll explain the many ways in which you can now invest in the various branches of alternatives. But for the moment, the more pressing questions are simply: what are the underlying ideas, and how do they make money?

Hedge Fund Strategies

....

As you know, the first hedge fund was started by Benjamin Graham in the Roaring Twenties. In those days secretive trading pools of superwealthy friends were all the vogue, and Graham's featured exactly the recipe you'd expect of the progenitor of value investing: he bought shares that he thought were undervalued, simultaneously shorting an equal amount of those he saw as too expensive. That way, he profited regardless of how the overall market moved. And that little trick is indeed what puts the hedge in hedge fund.

Here's an example. Let's say you love Ford, and you're sure it's the best car company out there. But you're worried about investing in it, because the overall market could crumble, taking everything down. OK, here's an idea: pick the car company you think is the worst one, say Lemon. Buy $1,000 worth of Ford stock, and sell $1,000 worth of Lemon short. You'll profit regardless of overall market direction, or even big news affecting the auto industry itself—so long as the market shares your view that Ford is superior to Lemon. Here's how.

Suppose the overall market (or just the car segment) advances. Both Ford and Lemon will go up. Thus, you'll make money on the Ford stock, your long, and lose money on Lemon, your short. However, so long as Ford goes up by *more* than Lemon does, which is certainly what you expect, your profit will exceed your loss.

If the market (or just the car segment) goes down, it works in reverse. You lose money on your Ford long, and make it on your Lemon short. But so long as Ford goes down less than Lemon does, you'll be ahead overall.

Just one last piece of the puzzle. Since we make money regardless of the overall market movements, this looks like a pretty low-risk bet; so we can ratchet up the returns with leverage. We might use our available cash to buy options instead of buying or selling the stock directly, or we could borrow to put on the trade.

Congratulations! You now understand the basic ideas behind most hedge strategies.

The first reference to a "hedge fund" appeared in a 1966 *Fortune* article by one Carol Loomis. In the nicely titled "The Jones Nobody Keeps Up With," she told the amazing story of Alfred Jones, who used strategies like this to generate fortunes for his investors. Little did she know that she was igniting a trend that now accounts for over $2 trillion of assets under management.

In the generation of hedge funds that grew up from that time until the advent of the more investor-friendly "liquid alternatives" described in the next chapter, the managers enjoyed many advantages over those operating in the traditional world. Unlike mutual funds, they faced no limits on shorting, leverage, or investing in nonstock assets. They kept their methods secret, revealing them not even to investors; took only the wealthiest clients, who agreed to keep their money invested for long periods; and, oh yeah, commanded those impressive fees.

If Benjamin Graham is Warren Buffett's hero, then Alfred Jones is an outright god to today's hedge fund managers. For he's the one who invented something much more dear to them even than the basic long/short idea: the 20% carried interest structure that has made so many so rich. Hedge fund managers typically get 2% of the assets under management every year as a management fee, but the big prize is that 20% of all the profits also go to the manager. Remember that the profits are driven not just by other people's money, but by leveraging up that money. If you get several hundred million under management (much less the billions that larger funds command), lever it, and do generate some real upside, 20% of the total profits is one heck of a payday.

Knowing a good thing when they see it, venture capital and private equity firms now charge the same way. So, all together: Here's to Alfred!

Since the '60s, many different hedge investing styles have emerged. The lines between them are a bit blurry, so that just about every source provides a somewhat different list. Nonetheless, the basic categories are pretty straightforward.

First, there are innumerable variations of the basic "pairs" trade, buying one security while selling another, across every sort of market. The offset might be accomplished by purchasing IBM on the one hand and selling the semiconductor sector index on the other; or by going long the S&P and shorting the FTSE; or buying the stock of the target in announced merger, and selling the stock of the acquirer. The basic idea is put to work in commodities, currencies, and just about any other class of securities you can imagine.

All of these are forms of betting on the *relative value* of two securities (or baskets of securities) rather than on the overall direction of markets, and so they carry the not terribly clever name "relative value" trades. If you're really equally balanced on the long and short side, another alias for this sort of fund is "market neutral."*

But what if the manager is actually bullish or bearish on the overall market? These folks are said to have a "bias," and their strategies are said to be "directional"—they're trying to benefit from market direction but are still taking both long and short positions as a hedge. The great majority of long/short funds do, in fact, have a long bias.

There are analogous strategies for the fixed income world. Although the basic ideas are the same, the execution can get mindblowingly complex. These managers are trying to exploit tiny pricing discrepancies in every sort of interest-related instrument, in the shape of comparative yield curves, and in the nooks and crannies of some of the most sophisticated derivatives in existence, like indexes of credit default swaps (where the famous J.P. Morgan "Whale" got beached).

The majority of hedge funds run some version of these kinds of strategies. But other funds specialize in quite different styles, and it's worth understanding those, too, for often they will generate meaningfully different returns under different market conditions. You'll see that in the graph that follows.

---

* Check out **dollar neutral** and **beta neutral** in the glossary.

CORRELATIVE RETURNS TO HEDGE FUND STRATEGIES

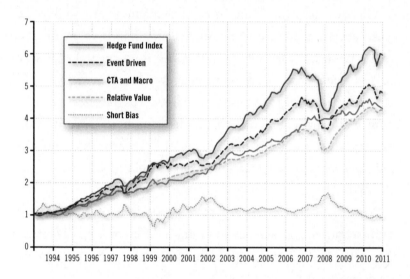

Source: Centre for Hedge Fund Research

Perhaps the most distinctive type of these strategies is called "global macro," home to the most successful and famous hedge fund managers of all time, like George Soros, Stanley Druckenmiller, and Ray Dalio. They've made fortunes for themselves and their investors betting on big-picture global trends rather than on the relative performance of specific stocks or bonds.

One thing you hear global macro guys argue about is whether some pending development has already been "priced in" to the market, meaning: do securities prices already reflect the impact of the potential event? For example, one might think: "The upcoming German elections will make a Eurozone breakup appear more likely. And if the euro collapses, the deutsche mark will become incredibly strong . . . so strong, that it'll make the cars they produce prohibitively expensive in the rest of the world. Let's short the German auto sector."

Global macro funds are of particular interest these days because governments are using such heavy hands to manipulate their economies. That makes traditional, fundamental analysis of interest rates, earnings, and business cycles less predictive of future securities prices than usual; and it reduces the effectiveness of many mathematical models that underlie numerous relative value strategies. On the other hand, predicting governmental policies, and how markets may react, is exactly what global macro guys like to do.

Nonetheless, as a category, the biggest allure of this style is its noncorrelation, its tendency to produce different kinds of returns than other investments, especially when those other investments are doing poorly. Take a look:

GLOBAL MACRO RETURN/S&P 500 RETURN, JANUARY 1997–MARCH 2012

Global macro has produced positive returns during the five worst quarters for the S&P since January 1997.

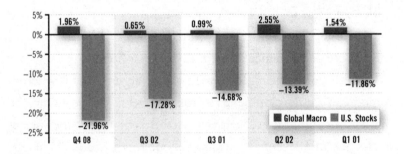

Source: Altegris

Those gains may not be so amazing from a gross return point of view, but when you're outpacing stocks by significant double digits, the comparative returns obviously look pretty darn good. This style is one of the better diversifying strategies out there.

Yet another kind of fund is called "event driven." These managers believe they see two things: an inherently mispriced security and a potential catalyst that will make its true value apparent. The most popular kind is "distressed" investing.

Most distressed investing concerns buying up debt of troubled issuers for small fractions of the face amount of bonds, and then working hard to maximize the payout. Appaloosa Management's David Tepper, perhaps the biggest star of this field, turned 400% profit in four months when he bought American Airlines bonds in the near panic that followed its filing for bankruptcy. When the dust settled, others caught on: the loans were likely to be paid after all. But Tepper wasn't finished; as is often true, the real idea was to eventually take over the company, because in bankruptcy proceedings the common stockholders are often wiped out, and the majority of the new equity is issued to the old bondholders.

Of course, you'd never see this sort of activity from traditional money managers (and you couldn't possibly in a passively managed ETF). If you want a good example of why it's possible for some funds to outperform the market, there you go.

Distressed investing also produces many of the more entertaining tales in finance; Elliott Capital versus Argentina reads like an adventure comedy plotline. And it explains why the Argentine president flies commercial when she's outside the country.

Paul Singer's New York–based Elliott Capital bought Argentine sovereign debt for pennies on the dollar just before the government defaulted in 2000. As happened more recently with

Greece, negotiations followed, by which nearly all the old creditors agreed to take new bonds in exchange for their old ones, absorbing a 70% loss in the process. But Elliott refused to budge, held on to its original bonds, and sued for payment in full. A New York judge agreed: Argentina still owed Elliott $1.6 billion.

Well, that's fine, but it's a bit tough for judges in Manhattan to compel a treasurer in Buenos Ares to do much of anything. So Elliott's lawyers started a great global goose chase, looking for Argentine assets in countries with courts that would be sympathetic. . . . Elliott almost nabbed the Argentine president's plane on a diplomatic trip to the United States, but the plot leaked, and the trip was canceled midflight. Amazingly, the fund got a judge in Ghana to order seizure of the pride of the Argentine navy, the *Libertad*, during a worldwide goodwill tour, when it stopped there for fuel. Elliott's demand for a $30 million ransom—er, payment—was foiled only by a decree, months later, of the International Tribunal of the Law of the Sea.

Maybe that's a good segue to another event-driven style, "activist" funds. These managers believe that if you want something done well, you should do it yourself. Many of these are like the old "corporate raider" guys: take a toehold in a stock and then launch a proxy fight or PR war urging the company management to increase value, say, by selling off a division (or, maybe, just resigning). Carl Icahn, the famous pioneer, is still active (recent target: Netflix); Dan Loeb of Third Point (Yahoo!); and Bill Ackman of Pershing Square (Herbalife) also keep CEOs up at night. "Operational activists" are the quieter side of this group, working collaboratively with existing management to improve a company's basic performance, increase productivity, reduce overhead, or maybe pursue acquisitions. If you've ever had a Snapple, you've tasted results by Nelson

Peltz and Trian Fund Management, probably the most famous of this breed.

Then there are a few classic arbitrage strategies to mention. **Merger arbitrage** players try to capture the "deal spread" between a target's current market price and the amount they expect an acquirer to actually pay. **Convertible arbitrage** is discussed in chapter 6. In an **index arbitrage**, traders seek to exploit tiny differences between the value of the basket of securities that make up an ETF, and the price of the ETF itself.

"Emerging" is emerging. That is, local hedge funds are springing up in several developing economies, which is certainly where everyone expects the growth to be over the next decade. For example, a few quality Chinese-based hedge funds have appeared over the past few years; there, and in other evolving societies, it doesn't take much imagination to believe that local managers might have a better grasp of the real opportunity set than does a macroeconomist sitting in New York.

Finally, one of my favorite kinds of funds: those that trade niche, inefficient markets. Take electricity trading. Most of the market participants there are not terribly price conscious, because utilities, after all, pass costs through to their users (that would be you). Instead, the big motivation, and career protection, is in ensuring against brownouts; if they overpay for capacity, so be it. Traders who only care about money—and can "source" megawatts—have an advantage.

So you can see why the phrase "hedge fund" is so ambiguous: it describes an awful lot of different styles. No wonder even industry insiders often pause for a moment before trying to answer that basic question: What's a hedge fund?

Private Equity and Venture Capital

···

There's equity, and then there's private equity.

The word *stocks* make most people think about owning microscopic pieces of enormous public enterprises. More sophisticated investors, however, imagine owning big chunks of private companies. Passive income is wonderful, and hard assets offer great inflation hedges; but for genuine wealth creation, nothing beats building a successful company of which you own a meaningful slice.

There are two categories of alternatives aimed at this goal: "private equity" and "venture capital." The potential rewards can be huge; a good PE or VC fund should return multiples of your investment, although you do have to wait a long time for that, maybe seven or even ten years. More or less, these funds are structured like hedge funds, with similar fees (details in chapter 10).*

Many sources lump PE and VC strategies together because they share the idea of owning big slices of nonpublic companies. But there are huge differences in what they do and how they do it.

Private Equity

It's hard to overstate the influence of PE firms on the U.S. economy: the various companies they own employ one of every twenty U.S. workers, through brands like Hilton, Lego, Toys"R"Us, Hertz, and Burger King. It's an enormous industry, but the big thing all PE investment styles have in common is making long-term bets in nonpublic companies (that's what's "private," not just

---

* Angel investors also chase venture investments and face longtime horizons, but normally invest directly into seed-stage companies rather than going through funds.

their clubs), and then taking very active management roles in the targets.

There's a trademark transaction of the PE field, rather like the way a long/short trade identifies hedge funds. It is the corporate version of a fixer-upper: buy up a troubled company in a deal called a "leveraged buyout," or "LBO," turn it around, and resell it. A different tack is to "roll up" many successful small companies together into a dominant industry juggernaut. A less common strategy is "growth capital," taking large stakes in successful young companies . . . like the Professional Bull Riders tour, which was bought by a PE shop a couple of years ago.

So exactly what makes LBOs, those famous corporate buyouts, work? *Barbarians at the Gate*–type stories are cool enough to make movies about, but we don't need Hollywood-caliber drama to make lots of dough. The idea is actually pretty simple, really just like that fixer-upper: buy with as big a mortgage as possible at the bottom of a cycle, do your repairs, and sell when the market improves. You, not the bank that loaned the money, get the benefit of the increased value.

Let's say there's a manufacturing company that's gone a bit to seed: the plant needs updating, the product is a bit outdated, the marketing plans ignore the Internet. Maybe the old managers and owners are even a bit tired themselves. The company is still profitable, but less so every year. Here you have an ideal private equity target.

First, the PE firm buys it for maybe four times earnings (a normal multiple for something with little growth). If the company had been making $10 million a year, that's a $40 million purchase price. Now, the big trick is to borrow as much of that as possible, minimizing the PE group's down payment. Maybe it puts up $8 million of cash, and borrows $32 million, to do the deal.

Let's next assume the PE firm invests another $8 million to upgrade equipment, brings in a hot young management team, and gets the marketing up to snuff. Things go well, and three years later the annual earnings have doubled to $20 million.

Time to sell. Now the earnings multiple is higher than when we bought it, because the business is growing (so-called multiple expansion). So maybe that's six times, not four, yielding a $120 million price tag. The loans are repaid from the proceeds—let's say that, with interest, the banks get back $40 million on their $32 million of loans, so they're quite happy. In fact, this type of loan business became so profitable that it gave birth to its own subcategory of PE investing, so-called mezzanine funds that specialized in financing other firm's buyouts.

OK. So here's our total: on a total of $16 million invested (the $8 million down payment, plus the fixer-up $8 million), the PE firm made a $64 million profit, 400%, in three years. Naturally, most of that goes back to the fund's investors, but the "20" of the "2 and 20" will mean a handsome $13 million or so to the fund's managers.

There you go. As you can see, management skill and hard work are crucial to success, but the secret to the outsize financial returns is in the leverage. The value of the profit improvement flowed to the PE firm, not to the banks who put up the great majority of the invested cash. Better to be a player in the value creation than just a spectator who's provided some of the capital.

Note that this whole plan goes an awful lot better in a good economy; if values are generally rising, buying a company on credit and selling it later tends to work, just like buying a home does.

The converse is what's happened to the deals done back in 2005 to 2008. The managers of those LBOs did a good job: a lower percentage of PE-owned companies went bust in the crash than on average. That's largely because the private equity folks saw what was coming and cut spending early. They also improved operations and kept sales steady. But they haven't really gotten rewarded for all their hard work, because of "multiple compression." They bought the companies at, say, eight times earnings in the frothy market but today can only sell them for, say, six times. So even if earnings are up 25%, they're not going to book a profit on a sale.

Like hedge funds, a bit of a negative connotation can hover around private equity. And also like hedge funds, there is sometimes a little fire to go along with all that smoke.

Here's the puffy purple around one eye of private equity. Some PE firms focus strictly on the "financial engineering" aspects of buyouts. They leverage the target company to the absolute hilt, and then have to rob the future of the company to pay off the debt. To make the payments, they might slash jobs that don't generate immediate revenues, eliminate R & D, and license away the valuable patents. On top of that, they might even charge the target company significant management fees, and cause it to dividend out any spare nickels they've otherwise missed. In this version of the game, there's no room for error. Many folks blame the bankruptcy of the beloved Harry & David on that kind of deal.

So, buyout-style PE is powerful stuff when done right, an example of real "alpha" generation through hard work and expertise. But it can be dangerous financial voodoo when greed rides too high.

"Roll-ups" work differently. In this variant, the idea is to coalesce a dominant company out of many scattered, independent businesses. There are usually "economy of scale" reasons to do that: better buying power; broader distribution; and more leverage off the same corporate infrastructure. There are also significant cost savings involved: you can typically cut out a lot of redundancies in systems, space, and, yes, people. Re/Max, now the nation's largest realty companies, is a great example . . . it is, of course, a confederation of thousands of independent businesses, now with lots of centralized and more efficient services. Many a large, successful company has been born of an accumulation of smaller ones in this way.

Maximizing the use of leverage, and therefore capturing as much value creation in the capital the firm invests, is usually at the root of PE profits. That can work very well in stable environments, but watch out during crises. Aside from choking off access to low-cost borrowing, sudden economic slowdowns lengthen the time needed to generate greater revenues, meaning improved sales might not be there in time to support the previously scheduled, higher debt service requirements. Oops.

That's one reason that the last crash was so cruel to this category, and something we'll bear in mind when we get around to portfolio construction.

Venture Funding

Now, for the sexy part of wealth creation through private companies: start-ups.

You know perfectly well that Mark Zuckerberg is now firmly planted in the list of the world's richest people, joining other famous founders like Bill Gates, Meg Whitman, Larry Page, Sergey Brin, Jerry Yang, Steve Case . . . well, let's just say it's a long list. But the angels and venture capitalists who provide the money to those folks did pretty darn well too. One, Reid Hoffman (himself on that list, thanks to LinkedIn and PayPal), injected $37,500 into Facebook's typical-looking angel round when the company sported a $5 million valuation. Let's see . . . that means his stock value grew to, uh, $75 million on the IPO date. Accel Partners invested well after Reid, in the company's first institutional round. Its $13 million still zoomed to $10 billion.

Ever since the first venture capital firm was started in 1946 by Georges Doriot—surprisingly, to encourage investment in start-ups by American soldiers returning from the war—venture deals have scored some of the most dramatic successes in the history of finance. For example, his firm's $70,000 investment in Digital Equipment Corporation grew to $355 million, a 500x gross return. Dell got started on $300,000 from friends and family.

Even taking those outsize performances into account, the averages have been pretty impressive. Over the last fifteen-year period, the average VC fund generated a 30% internal rate of return to investors.[*]

Of course, that included the great Internet boom, and shorter-term measures are less impressive. But such cycles are inevitable, and the pace of revolutionary change is only accelerating. Venture investing is undoubtedly a primary method for generating big, uncorrelated returns . . . if you pick the investments well.

How PE and start-up investors evaluate potential investments is very different, and very instructive. Since PE investments are in developed enterprises, the analysis is very data driven; formulas and spreadsheets rule, present values are constantly recalculated, variations in interest rate projections make or break a deal. PE investors expect every transaction to pay off at some level, even in their projected worst-case scenarios (which, of course, often turn out to be far better than the reality).

Venture investors couldn't be more different. They're investing in early-stage companies—sometime truly embryonic, sometimes ready

---

[*] Cambridge Associates.

for school—where the prospects are extremely uncertain. So, out of any ten investments, they hope for a homer or two; expect most to be in the break-even range; and know for sure that at least a couple will turn up snake eyes. (And if you look at all start-ups, rather than at just the professionally chosen ones, the total failure rate jumps to almost 50%.) That's why early-stage investors always want to see a potential for a 5x or 10x return on any given investment . . . the successful ones have a lot of work to do, carrying the load for lots of duds. We'll have a total drilldown on venture and angel investing later; meanwhile, it's always fun to fantasize about turning $37,500 into $75 million.

With private equity, big profits come from modest improvements multiplied by the magic of cheap borrowing. In venture, they come from innovation and giant business successes. At the end of the day, perhaps you don't really care about that difference, but that assumes you make it to the end of the day. As in any other financial endeavor, leverage is wonderful when it works, and poison when it doesn't: if the credit markets freeze, or you've miscalculated the cash available to pay debts, a PE deal is dead. For VCs, miscalculations are certainly still problematic, but at least the guillotine of debt is not hanging over the enterprise.

So those are the basics of the classic categories that dominate alternative investing. But as long as we're on the backstage tour, let's stop in for just a moment at two smaller studios where a couple of important but less popular shows are made.

Real Assets

What's real about real assets? They're physical, as opposed to financial.

If you want to know why they're so attractive these days, check out the following two charts. The first one shows the absolutely incredible stock appreciation of Warren Buffett's company, Berkshire Hathaway, over the past couple of decades.

BERKSHIRE HATHAWAY STOCK IN DOLLARS

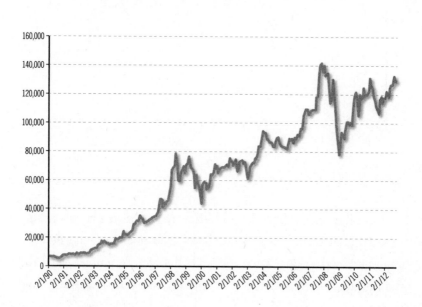

Source: Tangent Capital

But here is that same chart, with the company's price expressed in gold instead of dollars:

BERKSHIRE HATHAWAY STOCK IN OUNCES OF GOLD

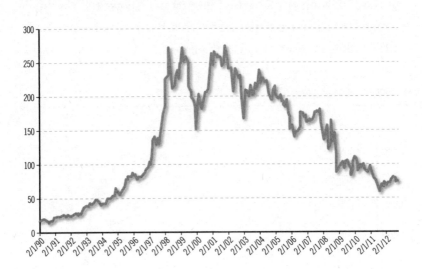

Source: Tangent Capital

In dollar terms, Berkshire Hathaway has been a runaway success. In gold terms, not so much, at least not since the Fed began sustained easing after the tech bubble. As currencies (and the financial assets measured by them) lose value, real assets hold theirs.

Other than gold, the most common "real assets" for investment include natural resources, art, timber, infrastructure, farmland, wine, collectibles, jewels, and various metals. We won't spend a lot of time on this category for the moment because the assets themselves don't require explanation, and whether and how to invest in them are discussed in chapters 8 and 9.

For now, just a few observations are in order. Aside from the obvious appeal of protecting against inflation, real assets are usually held outside the traditional financial system. For the doomsday crowd, that's another big plus, since a collapse of the banking system won't matter so much.

The trick, of course, is to make sure you don't need access to the cash you've got tied up in these assets when that crisis comes. Worse, if you've got leverage against the assets, and not enough cash or income to cover that debt, you'll wind up selling at horrendously depressed prices. That's actually just about the best way you can think of to destroy wealth, a lesson even the mighty Harvard endowment learned during the crash, when it suffered an $11 billion setback.

The core objection to most real assets is that they don't generate current income, a drawback most investors are willing to suffer to gain inflation protection. But there's a less obvious problem, too: in deflationary times, real assets lose value. You may believe that's a far-fetched concern, given the way the Fed's been running the printing press, but if you've been following Japan for the last twenty years you know you can't rule it out. We don't.

That's why some members of the real assets category are special. The first is timber. It does provide inflation protection, but it also generates annual income with a minimal amount of current investment, maintenance, or management . . . and that helps a lot in deflationary periods. Over time, of course, it also replenishes itself; and it provides a backdoor play to emerging economies because they all use wood as they develop. We'll return to this very interesting asset class later.

Another is infrastructure, like bridges and power generation plants. These generate returns over long periods from user fees, royalties, rents, and shares of government tax income. The good news, and the bad, is that you usually have a governmental partner: that can provide monopoly power, but also some uncertainty . . . politicians have been known to change their minds on occasion.

And finally, amid our discussion of the more exotic alternatives, let's talk about one surprise candidate for the category: TIPS, Treasury Inflation Protected Securities. Yes, I know, a financial security doesn't look much like the other members of the real asset family . . . but this one's adopted.

Sophisticated investors consider TIPS a real asset because they behave like one: in case inflation takes hold, these bonds compensate by automatically paying out more principal at maturity. So you can own them without fear of loss based on rising rates. And, of course, there is zero credit risk involved, unless you think the government itself will collapse. So while they pay effectively nothing in income right now, they are truly the ultimate inflation hedge.

On top of that, TIPS also have a very amazing special trick that makes them the rarest bird in the investment aviary. But to learn about that, you'll have to hang on for the more complete description coming in chapter 8.

Managed Futures

Futures have long been on the periphery for traditional investors for a darn simple reason: they do not provide an immediate ownership interest in an underlying asset.

Instead, one contracting party is agreeing to buy something, and the other to sell it, at a future date . . . but for a price agreed on today. So, for example, you and I might enter a contract under which you agree to pay me $35,000 for 50,000 pounds of cotton #2 (meaning, of "strict low middling" quality and a $1^2/_{32}$-inch fiber length) that I agree to deliver to you next October in Memphis, Tennessee. Once you see that example, you can guess why they evolved: so that farmers could know what they'd be able to get for a crop after harvest, and so figure out whether it was worth planting.

But you're agreeing to pay me, and I promise to deliver, several months from now. So the obvious question is how to ensure both sides make good on the deal. To address this, the exchanges that trade the contracts require deposits from both sides, and each must keep margin accounts available so that as the contract price moves over time, more capital can be drawn as necessary. As a result, at inception, you can control a $35,000 cotton contract for something like a $5,000 deposit—huge inherent leverage.

As the calendar progresses, you can then sell the contract at any time, which is the main idea these days—not a lot of traders take their trucks down to the docks. Now, imagine that we did our deal on Monday, and that by Friday the price of cotton has gone up from 70 cents to 80 cents. Suddenly, that $35,000 contract is worth $40,000; you could sell and pocket a cool 100% profit on the $5,000 of cash invested for five days. Who needs Vegas?

Today, futures contracts cover just about every sort of asset you can think of, a dizzying array of physical commodities and financial instruments: from the infamous pork bellies to currencies; from frozen orange juice to zinc; from propane to T-bills. It's a big field in which these traders frolic.

So that's the "futures" part. The "managed" part refers to the folks who do the investing in these things on behalf of their clients, so-called commodities trading advisors, or CTAs for short. The big thing to know about them is that the vast majority use complex computer programs to identify and then trade price trends with all sorts of arcane long, short, spread, and volatility strategies. The algorithms that dictate those trades are at the heart of the industry. Indeed, most managers call themselves "trend followers": as a simplistic example, once they see copper begin to rise, the programs kick in to buy, and will keep buying until some fancy math indicates that the trend has almost run its course.

That style makes the entire managed futures space a bit controversial. Some market pros think these trend-following systems are easy to exploit from the other side, with countertrend systems; and some others make the more general point that trend following can't work well in whipsaw markets.

Nonetheless, the record does show that these strategies do have a low correlation to traditional investments. They were up about 20% in the stock market crash of 2008. Much more impressive, they've also been up in ten of the last eleven big stock downturns, dating back to 1987, and flat in that eleventh one. A further highlight of the noncorrelation of managed futures is that their performance is not even closely correlated to the underlying assets to which they relate; that is, a metals trader may do well even if the metals markets don't. No doubt, like hedge fund strategies, that's because of the disparate long, short, spread, and volatility strategies deployed by CTAs.

The upshot is that managed futures do tend to zig when other investments zag. That in itself is a useful characteristic, one to which we'll return in the chapter about risk-reducing strategies.

In Review

All hedge funds share two traits: they trade in liquid securities, and they practice active risk management. Managers often pair a "long" position with a "short" one, trying to profit regardless of overall market moves, and use significant leverage to magnify the returns.

Here's a quick reference guide that shows the traditional way of categorizing alternatives.

Income Stream	Hedge Funds	Private Equity	Venture Capital	Managed Futures	Real Assets
Royalties	Equity Long/Short	Buyouts	Seed	Programatic	Gold
Rents	Credit Long/Short	Growth Cap	Late	Discretionary	Art
Mortgages	Event Driven	Emerging	Multi		Timber
Equipment Leasing	Distressed	Mezzanine			Farmland
ILS	Global Macro	Micro			Collectibles
Loans	Emerging	Natural Resources			Commodity
Specialty	Niche				Infrastructure
	Market Neutral				TIPS
	Stat Arb				
	Activist				

But, to make the book as useful as possible, we instead organize the subjects according to what various strategies can do for investors, like so:

Income (Job 1)	Risk Reduction (Job 2)	Return Enhancement (Job 3)	Purchase Power Protection (Job 4)
MLPs	Long/Short	Global Macro	Timber
Royalties	Arbitrage	Distressed	Gold
Peer-to-Peer	Funds of Funds	Activist	Water
Mezz/BDCs	Farmland	Venture Funds	RE Sponsor Equity
Specialty	Managed Futures	Angel	Art
Cat Bonds	Black Swan	O&G Drilling	TIPS
Multi-ETFs	Global Blue Chips	PE Secondaries	Infrastructure
EM Debt	Inefficient Markets	Growth PE	Collectibles

One noteworthy style is global macro, where managers bet on top-down macro trends, like sovereign credit risk or commodity prices. In distressed and activist investing, managers usually take a hands-on approach to facilitating change at the companies in which they've invested.

Private equity and venture capital managers, by contrast, normally focus on owning big chunks of private companies, positions that can't be sold on a moment's notice.

The signature PE trade is to buy a mature company with as much leverage as possible, fix it up, and sell it for a higher price. The next biggest variation involves "rolling up" many smaller companies into one big one.

Venture capital funds, and individual angels, invest in much-earlier-stage companies. A high level of uncertainty means some will completely fail, some will break even, and a few will be rockets.

Real assets offer the kind of long-term protection against currency devaluation and inflation that most paper assets simply cannot. A few also provide current income.

"Managed futures," the most enigmatic category of all, involves a CTA ("commodities trading advisor") running mathematical models to trade futures contracts on anything from pork bellies to Bunds. These strategies have tended to act as good diversifiers to traditional stock and bond portfolios.

Final Thought

Don't let the whiz-bangy names of these approaches mystify you, intimidate you, or cause you to pay higher fees than necessary to use them. Over the next several chapters we'll explain exactly what they can do for you, how to evaluate them and get what you pay for, which might perform best over time, and where to find specific choices.

CHAPTER 4

....

Major Alternative Structures

Form ever follows function.
—Louis Sullivan

A flood of marketing materials about new alternatives products is inundating investors. Much concerns the new "liquid" alternatives coming to market, a trend that, overall, is certainly a very good thing indeed. But often the related sales literature tosses around mysterious and out-of-context phrases like "the efficient frontier" and "core and satellite." It all sounds a bit like a random lecture by a spacey professor.

Investors are often left puzzled. Enjoyed the class, thanks . . . but, now what?

So in this chapter, we'll do a couple of things. We'll explain how those new liquid alternatives work, and compare them to both traditional private placements and another very interesting new option called "registered privates." And we'll provide some SparkNotes on what those academics are saying.

In choosing among alternative investment vehicles, the key question for most people will indeed turn on that liquidity issue— the ability to sell or redeem at any time is an enormous advantage, no doubt (and the typically lower fees don't hurt, either). After all, you've got to ensure your basic liquidity needs can be met in any market downturn or new system failure.

The decision is not, however, quite the no-brainer you might expect. As you'll see, to get that liquidity you may well have to trade away some expected performance. As in the real world of business, sometimes the best job candidates require long-term employment contracts.

After a quick tour of the big structures, we'll get to exactly what it is those oft-quoted professors are saying about allocating to alternatives. As you'll see, when it comes to picking investments, our take is that basic common sense can be more effective than differential equations.

Liquidity

It's not possible to overstate the importance of liquidity management in a portfolio. The very worst thing that can happen to an investor is forced liquidation of assets at the same time everyone else is doing the same thing. That's the surest way in the world to make a small fortune . . . from a large one.

The flip side is also true. As in sports and warfare, great defense often translates into fantastic offensive opportunities. If the markets come unglued and you have liquidity when others don't, you'll have unparalleled opportunities to truly ratchet up your wealth. Ask Warren Buffett: if you're prepared for crises, they're absolutely wonderful! Nonetheless, like any good thing, you actually can have too much liquidity, for many of the best investment opportunities simply cannot be instantly sold or redeemed.

Not all nontraded vehicles will force you to park your money for the same periods of time, and the differences are important. For example, although hedge funds typically require lockups, they're pretty short, usually a year . . . not so different from bank CDs. Let's call such investments "semiliquid." On the other hand, real assets certainly can't be sold instantly, but usually can be sold over a period of two or three years. That probably qualifies as "illiquid." But even further out on the scale, many private equity funds not only require very long-term lockups (as much as ten years), but also may require ongoing funding commitments for both the investment commitment and fee payments. Hmmm . . . that actually may manage to qualify as "antiliquid."

It's extremely important, too, to understand that even profound illiquidity can definitely have its rewards. That's valuable to remember right now, when everyone is demanding liquid options for everything. The memories of 2008 are fresh, and its impact completely skewed the target asset allocation percentages of many institutional investors. As a result of this **denominator effect**, they are still avoiding new private equity and real estate deals, and still shedding positions in older ones at bargain prices.

More sellers than buyers means the so-called illiquidity premium is high right now. There are, simply, good deals to be had for investors who can comfortably sock away chunks of their assets for several years. An investor with $10 million who burns only a few hundred thousand per year on his lifestyle may sleep better at night because he's fully liquid; but his heirs are sneaking Ambien. Maybe they could tell him a bedtime story about Columbia University.

Columbia had been around for sixty-three years when rivals Hamilton and Union were founded in 1817. The new guys had the connections, though, and legislators favored them with a whopping $240,000 in cash to get them started. The bitterly complaining elder institution was awarded a professor's overgrown garden as compensation, valued at a meager $10,000 . . . with the caveat that the school could not sell or use it for commercial purposes. Now, that's the definition of illiquid.

Stuck with the plot for a hundred years, the school eventually won the right to lease it out, and did finally find a nice family willing to rent it. They were called the Rockefellers, and they proceeded to build their signature landmark complex there after clearing out the weeds. That land lease provided essentially all of the school's operating income for many decades, until the old garden was finally sold in 1985 for . . . $400 million. That formed the core of the school's endowment, which, after being invested in a very panoramic portfolio since then, is now valued around $9 billion.

Sweet dreams.

"You get what you pay for."

Now, I've never thought that was right . . . gee, haven't you overpaid for lots of things? Right now, it's certainly very easy to overpay for average hedge fund managers, running average strategies, performing averagely well. But there's no need to. A huge raft of new liquid alternatives, featuring much lower fees and full liquidity, are leading the charge toward full democratization of alternative strategies.

But, as we start that discussion, let's remember that there is an accurate version of that old saying, too, which goes like this: "You don't get what you don't pay for." There are still many truly outstanding hedge, venture, and private equity fund managers out there who do deliver the goods—that is, returns, *after fees*, that provide honest-to-goodness alpha. As in any other field, however, top talent doesn't come cheap. So, while it's definitely true that not every hedge fund charging full freight fees is being run by a George Soros, it is also true that he's not exactly going to drop his current gig to manage a mutual fund for the typical half of 1%, either.

These key points—that liquid alternatives are extremely attractive investments for many purposes, but that nontraded vehicles are the only options for access to certain strategies and many top managers—are worth drilling into before moving on to the issue of matching up alternative strategies to the jobs you need done.

Alpha into Beta

You already know that alpha is the holy grail of money managers (and investors!). Whatever technical definition you like, it boils down to genuine value creation above **beta**, the return produced by an unmanaged investment in that same asset class. That takes tremendous amounts of hard work and, usually, an edge of some sort: an information advantage, proprietary deal flow, something.

(One fantastic fund of funds manager, whose job is to allocate money to the best strategies he can find, likes to relate the number-one response he gets from the many dozens of new managers he interviews each year. In answer to "So, tell me, what's your edge?," the most common response is: "My edge? I was top of the class at Princeton." Well, thanks for playing, but that doesn't count.)

The most basic reason that a true edge is necessary is those 9,000 managers. Anything that can be copied, gets copied. The alpha gets commoditized. As the head of one of the best firms out there, AQR, says: "Today's alpha is tomorrow's beta." In some ways, of course, that's not terrible news for average investors, since once that happens broadly enough the idea can usually be accessed in liquid form; but, of course, by that time it's also lost most of its punch.

Naturally, managers therefore try to keep winning strategies very quiet, which can lead to an entertainingly paranoid cult of secrecy at top firms. One elite manager, Bridgewater, is rather famously proud of its Big Brother, CIA-like environment, squirreled away in the deep woods of Connecticut with hidden video recorders and cell phone blockers in every room. Slightly crazy, maybe, but given the track record, who's to argue?

Bridgewater is one of those exceptions that proves the rule. Generally, as successful managers grow, their strategies get replicated, and their edge gets dulled as others pile in to previously profitable trades. Except for the very rarest of traders, scale is the enemy of alpha.

Study after study shows that, in general, smaller hedge funds perform better than the multibillion-dollar behemoths. Of course this makes total sense: it is easier to find an edge in a niche strategy (say, electricity trading) than it is in a multibillion-dollar long/short stock fund. It is easier to maintain an edge when you hold a knowledge advantage in a subset of a field (medical devices) than a broader one (health care).

Indeed, in nearly every meeting in which a promising hedge fund manager explains his style to a potential investor, a very early question back is: How much "capacity" does the strategy have? How much money can it absorb before the manager's edge no longer works? "Hundreds of millions" is a typical response, maybe a couple of billion, tops . . . almost nobody says "unlimited" with a straight face.

The plain fact is that smaller and midsize hedge funds are the best places to look for alpha. As always, there are a tiny handful of exceptions, a few folks who do make it work with many billions under management. In this industry, too, you'll find a LeBron James or Meryl Streep . . . people who dominate their professional peers, earn outrageous incomes, and totally deserve it. You just won't find that many.

Alpha lives best, and for much longer periods, when it's based on something that just can't be copied, like work and entrepreneurial talent, where there's no secret formula that will eventually escape into the wild and reproduce until the food supply is exhausted. That's exactly why you find so much of it away from the lightning-fast world of publicly traded securities, machine-based trading, and totally liquid investments. Sustainable alpha is not really so much about "beating" the system with some sort of genius idea, because the system usually self-corrects for that. It's more about "using" the system to take advantage of skills and experience.

The Crossroads

This brings us to the critical crossroads in alternative investing: "liquid alternatives" versus the traditional, unregistered, privately placed variety. The former now offer tremendous opportunities for average investors, including important new income options and a variety of choices that mimic traditional hedge fund strategies. The latter are the classic, old-school hedge, venture and private equity funds where most of the best managers hang out. And then there's a brand-new entry that's hitting the charts with a bullet, something called a "registered private."

Liquid Alternatives: Mutual Funds, ETFs, and the Gang

Liquid alternatives are a revolutionary advance for average investors. The term refers to alternative assets and strategies that are packaged up inside mutual funds, ETFs, publicly traded partnerships, and a few other vehicles that can be bought by anyone and either sold or redeemed at any time.

Many alternative income-generating products come in these packages. They're discussed in the next chapter; for now, suffice it to say that, as compared to traditional fixed income products, these can provide higher yields, inflation protection, and tax benefits. Another group of liquid alternatives, but most famously the gold ETF, offers exposure to real assets that most investors would otherwise find impossible to hold.

But the most exciting, and rapidly developing, branch of liquid alternatives is the "smart beta" category, which provides easy, low-cost access to traditional hedge fund strategies.

They're "smart" because they limit risk. The category is dominated by long/short stock strategies that should comfortably outperform long-only strategies during choppy and down markets. Other styles provide noncorrelation: managed futures, various arbitrage strategies, global macro, and even currencies. All are extra smart because the fees associated with them are typically far less than those charged by the traditional privately placed funds that historically ran these strategies.

They're "beta" because . . . well, that's what you're going to get. It's a great marketing pitch to say you're running a hedge style in a large, liquid fund, but *investment style alone most certainly does not generate alpha*. Investors in most "alternative" mutual funds and ETFs should simply not expect to see it—it is essentially impossible to generate alpha at scale, with total liquidity, within tight constraints on asset classes, strategies . . . and manager fees.

Now, you might just be thinking: wait, isn't beta exactly what I don't want to pay for? But here we're talking about strategies that provide powerful risk-adjusted exposure to the stock market and powerful diversification benefits. That's worth paying (some-thing) for . . . what you do not want to do is pay for alpha and get beta. With these, you don't.

Just as with privately placed alternatives funds, *managers mat-ter hugely* in liquid alternative products, much more than they do in the long-only world. Of course, even great strategy doesn't do you much good if there's a mediocre team executing it. And, given the recent breakneck race toward liquid alternatives, the manager quality level is bound to be uneven. So avoid swooning over the general description and drill down on the track record. With any alternative product, performance statistics are more important than a brand name.

Also, recall that there are many alternative strategies that are simply beyond the reach of mutual funds and ETFs, which face legal limits on use of leverage, short selling, and holding il-liquid assets. In addition, liquidity requirements preclude smart beta products from pursuing some strategies that just take time to work, like distressed or activist investing, and also from pursuing private equity and real asset styles.

A NOTE ON CLOSED-END FUNDS

For the sake of completeness, we'll briefly mention closed-end funds here. Normally, they don't belong in an alternatives discussion because the majority hold very standard income instruments, like municipal bonds. However, CEFs can invest in more illiquid assets than can traditional open-end mutual funds, which opens the door to some alternative-style assets, like mezzanine debt and asset-backed loans.

Significantly, the structure of the closed-end fund means that there can be, and usually is, a difference between the fund's net asset value (the "NAV") and its traded price: the securities inside the fund might be worth $100/share, but the shares might trade at $80, or even $120. Be careful buying CEFs at huge premiums to NAV, for that premium can collapse very quickly; and do not buy at a discount in the belief that the share value will return to the NAV—usually, discounts stay in a fairly consistent zone over time, and can even increase. Finally, avoid IPOs of closed-end funds; they frequently lose value in the first weeks after launch, as the costs of the offering are factored into the asset base.

Traditional Private Placements

As mentioned in the previous chapter, hedge, private equity, and venture capital strategies have historically been available only through "private placements" of limited partnership interests. That's the biggest reason why they've seemed so exotic: they were, effectively, doubly unavailable to average investors.

First, private placements were indeed private, and couldn't be generally advertised or offered to the public . . . they could be exposed only to wealthy individuals who already had a relationship with the fund managers or brokers. So unless you were a select member of a pretty fancy circle, you would never have known they existed. It wasn't until 2012 that legislative changes eliminated this restriction. That's why you're seeing ads for these things now, but never did before.

But maybe not hearing about them was no real loss . . . they usually required huge minimum investments, sometimes as much as $10 million, and were typically sold only to "qualified purchasers," institutions, and individuals with a $5 million net worth. Even now, after all the recent changes, private placements can still be purchased only by "accredited investors," generally those with a $1 million net worth excluding their residence.

Secret deals with huge capital commitments: not exactly for the Elks Club.

Nonetheless, hedge funds rocketed in the '90s as the technology and communications revolutions made arbitrage opportunities between world markets easier to see and exploit. To take full advantage, you needed really smart people, some computers, not too much regulation, and lots of leverage . . . and all were present. The combination generated volcanoes of money, to which rich folks, as is their wont, gravitated rapidly. The clubby exclusivity only made the game more appealing.

That, in turn, led to a talent exodus from the traditional Wall Street institutions that still stings. After all, why work at some schleppy bank for a few hundred thou when you could make tens of millions, or more, managing a hedge fund? That is why, today, we have those 9,000 hedge funds of this traditional "private placement" kind (and maybe 7,000 too many). That is also why privately placed funds is where you'll find the most talented money managers in the world.

Private placements certainly have drawbacks. Beyond that famous fee structure, they usually require some sort of minimum investment period, or **lockup**, and may also have **gates** that prevent investors from leaving even after that period expires.*

Moreover, as you no doubt are aware, privately placed hedge funds haven't exactly been the darlings of the media lately, and for

---

* An unfortunate recent example involved the widely held Endowment Fund, which notified long-standing investors in late 2012 that subsequent withdrawals would be limited (but not the fees on the money stuck inside).

good reason: some high-profile insider trading cases and, rarely but spectacularly, episodes of outright fraud. (Frankly, not so surprising when you think about it: combine enormous money and utter secrecy and you have con artist heaven.) The reality, however, is that such issues shouldn't overly worry reasonably careful investors. As a practical matter, totally standard due diligence tips (like, ensuring the fund's assets are held by an independent custodian, and that top accounting and law firms are involved—steps outlined in chapter 10) provide solid protection. In addition, the Dodd-Frank Act now requires that most managers register with the SEC, which has begun monitoring and auditing them.

So, yes, there are issues. But there are also reasons why the vast majority of the world's top investors hold huge percentages of their assets in privately placed hedge, PE, and venture funds. Many managers do indeed produce alpha, even in the most highly competitive markets, and many of the best alternative strategies, especially those involving private companies and real assets, just don't lend themselves to liquid alternatives. For all their warts, old school private placements definitely have a place in many portfolios.

The New Kid: Registered Privates

If liquid alternatives are too hot, and traditional private placements are too cold, there's a new entry on the scene that might be like the baby bear's porridge: just right. A "registered private" might suit you quite well.

We just mentioned that most investment *managers* must now be registered with the SEC, but that's a separate question than whether the privately placed *funds* they manage are. Even if the manager is registered, the actual vehicle in which you invest might or might not be. And a registered investment *fund* must have layers of investor protections that unregistered ones need not. Most notably, these include an independent board to oversee the manager, an independent custodian to hold its funds, and prohibitions on certain transactions with affiliates. Those mechanics are a key reason why liquid alternative funds—which are all registered—are allowed to be sold to the public.

"Registered privates" provide these protections, too. As the name implies, they are sold only through private placements . . . and so, to accredited investors only. But they offer many advantages to traditional private placements aside from those additional investor protections. First, because they can have an unlimited number of investors, they allow hedge, PE, and venture firms to accept much lower investment minimums than they will in traditional private placements. Second, most carry lower fees, require shorter lockups, and offer better liquidity than traditional private placements. And third, you can invest in them through IRAs, which many private placements don't allow.*

Registered privates have advantages over liquid alternatives, too, because they aren't constrained by the same investment limitations as mutual funds. Thus, they can invest in less liquid securities, and management can pursue the kinds of distressed and activist styles that they can't with liquid alternatives. Indeed, registered privates can run nearly any hedge, venture, or PE strategy.

From an investor's point of view, there is very little not to like about registered privates. Given a choice between two investments with similar quality managers running similar strategies, where one option is a registered private and the other is a classic private

---

* Technically, as registered vehicles, the holdings don't count as "plan assets" under ERISA.

placement, it would be hard to choose the latter. You can expect to see more of them in the future, as the only real drawback is that, as compared to traditional private placements, they do involve additional fees, legal hassles, and reporting requirements. But those are headaches for the managers, not the investors.

The Panoramic, Risk-Tolerant Portfolio, Continued

Filling the jobs you need done with investment opportunities listed in the next four chapters, and with a close watch on personal liquidity, is the primary way most investors will approach alternative investing. But, as we mentioned at the top, nearly all the marketing materials you'll see for liquid alternatives products feature some pretty fancy academic rationales for why you should be in them. So if you're up for a little extra-credit work, stick around.

However, if this sort of stuff just isn't your cup of tea, there's no need to be polite. You'll notice how near we are to the end of the chapter, so feel free to motor on to the inventory of alternative income sources in chapter 5.

Modern Portfolio Theory and Asset Allocation

As you know, **modern portfolio theory**, or MPT, has been the reigning investment dogma for decades, taught in economics classes and business schools everywhere. Its founders include Harry Markowitz and William Sharpe, whose Nobels show they definitely had a clue.

I'm sure you've heard the basic ideas, like the famous "rational investor" who keeps markets efficient, instantly reflecting all available information so that prices are always "right" at any given moment. (Remember, it is not polite to shout "Facebook IPO!" during class.)

Therefore, the argument goes, betting on movements of particular stocks is a game of pure chance, and because of brokerage and management fees, it's a loser over time. The whole thing is very much like playing roulette: black and red turn up wholly randomly, and because only the house wins on the zeros, every gambler loses if he sticks around long enough. Experts (and casino owners) call that certainty the "gambler's ruin."

But for our purposes, the more important point concerns MPT's ideas on how to blend investments together. Markowitz's big insight was that an investment should not be judged by its own characteristics alone, but rather by how it impacts the overall risk and return of the combination of securities an investor holds. It's all part of the search for the mathematically ideal portfolio, the heavenly "efficient frontier."

And here it is, the sensuous curve that is the erogenous zone of the investment world. If Helen Gurley Brown had edited *Barron's* instead of *Cosmo*, it would have been on every cover.

EFFICIENT FRONTIER

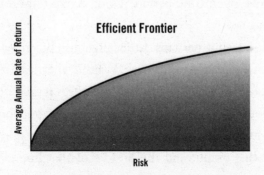

This is the place where the best constructed portfolios reside: those that maximize the gain you can achieve at whatever level of risk you take, or, flip side of the same coin, minimize the risk for a given level of returns.

The graph works like this. The vertical axis is "annual return" and the horizontal one is "risk" (also known as "standard deviation" or "volatility"). Any combination of those two features can be plotted. The idea, however, is that all opportunities actually available in the real world fall within the dark space. The white area is where higher return/lower risk opportunities would be if they existed, but they don't. So we want the portfolio, as a whole, to reside on the border between light and dark—again, where we get the greatest possible return per unit of risk. Eminently sensible.

But perhaps you're wondering how it's possible to measure "units of risk" so precisely; certainly I did the first time I saw this. What the professors really mean by that is: "least expected volatility in the investment." They equate riskiness of an investment with its historical volatility, and if you want to remember one key idea of modern portfolio theory, that's the one.

Now, how to find your way to the efficient frontier? The plan is to combine individual securities in a way that tamps down overall portfolio volatility, because their performances will balance each other out in a given time period. Voilà! Same total return + less "risk" = nirvana.

Sounds good but perhaps rather obvious. But maybe it's not, for here's an interesting question: Why is that line curved and not straight? Well, imagine just two securities represented by two points. If you just connected them, of course, you would indeed get a straight line. But combine the two inside a portfolio represented in this graph, and the middle of that line gets nudged upward a bit, because total return stays the same, but the risk goes down. The resulting "hump"—the space between the new curve and what otherwise would be a straight line—is the "free ride" you earn by diversifying.

All quite neat and tidy, eh? Well, so was physics before Einstein. Back then, Newton's clockwork formulas were reliable, the big issues were solved, and physics was just a matter of mopping up some nits. As it turned out, however, those little details happened to include relativity, quantum mechanics, and some practical results like nuclear weapons.

Something like that has happened in the investing world, too. A plethora of exceptions started creeping into modern portfolio theory, and then one blew a giant hole in it: behavioral economics, our interesting friend from chapter 2. Whereas MPT is all about rational investors, efficient markets, and elegant formulas, behavioral economics is about real humans, irrational prices, and messy emotions. The two schools of thought are ying and yang, sun and moon, Jekyll and Hyde. And while the new field hasn't exactly yielded a nuclear explosion, the financial implosion in 2008 was close enough for most investors.

When behavioral economics is ascendant, strategies based on efficient markets do terribly. "Relative value" and "mean reversion" trades, which depend on securities prices gravitating to some intrinsic values or historic norms, get crushed.

Just one example to illustrate: a pretty classic hedge fund strategy compares the price of securities inside a "closed-end fund" to the price of the fund itself. Usually these funds do trade at a discount to the total price of all the securities in it, the so-called net asset value. That discount falls within a very well defined historical norm, say 3% to 7%. So when the fund sells at only a 3% discount, traders would sell the fund and buy the stocks; they'd reverse the trade when the price fell to around a 7% discount, buying the fund and selling the stocks. And because the trade was so historically reliable, but not super profitable, traders took out big leverage to stoke their returns.

You can probably guess what happened in '08. When the crisis hit, everyone sold the funds to raise cash, just like they did anything else that had a market. Suddenly the difference between a fund's price and the NAV of the securities it held jumped to 10%, 15%, even 25%. For those desperate to sell, the price just didn't matter that much, and certainly the historic spread between NAV and fund shares didn't matter at all. None of the models was prepared, and funds playing the strategy were crushed, falling by a third while the managers were out having lunch.

Strategies based on security prices moving toward their "inherent value" simply don't function when the stampede for the door breaks out. Moreover, many "better" assets get sold first, simply because they have the most ready buyers . . . in those cases, relative value trades worked in exactly the opposite way than anyone would have reasonably expected. A mirror phenomenon punished many better hedge fund managers themselves: well-run funds met requests to redeem out their investors, while less-prepared funds threw up gates and imprisoned theirs.

That's why the Great Investing Schism—the split between MPT and behavioral economics—really does remind you of that split between Newtonian physics and relativity. Normally, the principles of modern portfolio theory are close enough to true. Our usual investing experience is "Newtonian": standard investment models work pretty well; historical patterns hold up; and outliers revert to the mean.

But sometimes just the opposite is true. Markets seize up, tempers flare, panic reigns. Mr. Hyde arrives. The managers who excel are those who play big-picture supply-and-demand trends instead of delicate historical patterns: what would people, in their full-on emotional mode, acting in inefficient markets, buy and sell?

Even absent such crisis periods, there's a profound question about whether the market really constantly and efficiently prices "information" into stocks, as MPT holds. From what I can tell, it sure does seem that, for example, some global macro managers are just better than other people at putting new data into perspective and understanding the trading consequences.

In fact, this core concept of MPT—that all information is instantaneously and accurately baked into the markets—appears at odds with the real human tendencies to perceive information differently, depending on how, when, and to whom it is presented.

In a study done at Harvard Medical School a few years back, students were told about two different treatment options for a certain cancer: surgery or radiation. Over five years, surgery had the better outcome, but of course there are always risks in operating. About those risks, half the students were told that the operation had a 90% survival rate after one month. The others were told that the operation has a 10% mortality risk during the first thirty days. You'll recognize that the students are being told the same thing in two different ways. But when asked how they would go about treating their patients, 83% of the first group said they would recommend surgery, but only half of the second group said they would.

In this literally life-and-death decision, made by super-smart people, the framing of the question changed the outcome. If you ask the question with the emphasis on the positive, talking about survival, you get a lot more buy-in than you do when stating it negatively, highlighting mortality.

Likewise, identical economic information, presented through different media filters, has disparate impacts on markets and traders. If unemployment numbers rise, but less than the consensus forecast, some media report it as a "jump"; others will still call the rate "lower than expected." Our stiff, buttoned-up rational investor is actually quite a dancer, gyrating away to the tunes of a band called the Perceptions.

So don't get hypnotized by the academics, and be wary of men in suits who keep repeating "efficient frontier" while slowly waving a prospectus back and forth. You can't predict the future from past events. But that hardly renders us helpless to prepare.

As we just discussed, most MPT-based investing approaches rely on securities prices "converging" on some implicit or expected value; they are "convergent" strategies. But as you also know, other managers, like global macro guys, are much more concerned about top-down thinking and basic supply-and-demand trends—they're more in the behavioral economics camp. Because this group of strategies is pretty much exactly the opposite of bottoms-up, MPT styles, we'll call them "divergent."

Divergent strategies have tended to perform well when convergent ones haven't. "Managed futures" funds were up 20% in the crash. The best global macro managers did incredibly well then, too, by betting on falling stock indexes and rising sovereign bonds without regard to any historical patterns. And the guys who really cleaned up, like John Paulson ($5 billion, personally), had gone so far as to directly bet against the historical patterns built into the black box models followed by so much of Wall Street. None of these profitable trades would have been picked up by traditional, MPT, "convergent" strategies.

So, there's a core idea: a test of whether a portfolio is uncorrelated, and therefore risk-tolerant, is whether it contains both convergent and divergent strategies.

In Review

Liquid alternatives change the investing landscape in much the same way as the advent of mutual funds did. "Smart beta" and alternative income strategies can be accessed through these low-fee, fully transparent, registered and regulated vehicles.

"Registered privates" lack daily liquidity but offer many investor protections as compared to traditional private placements. They cover many kinds of strategies that liquid alternatives cannot.

Old-school private placements have downsides regarding lockups and fees, but the format is the best fit for many venture capital, real asset, and private equity strategies, and is where most of the best managers reside.

Don't get hypnotized by the academics behind modern portfolio theory. There's no predicting the future from the past. But reducing risks through maximal strategy and asset diversification remains a good plan.

"Divergent" strategies tend to zig when the more traditional "convergent" strategies start to zag. In periods of high system stress, the latter often fail, and the former perform better.

Final Thought

Liquid alternatives really are great, but they are not *always* better. Old-school private placements are still where you'll find most of the best overall returns.

CHAPTER 5

Higher, Inflation-Protected Current Income (Job 1)

MLPs	Royalties	Peer to Peer	Mezz/BDCs
Specialty	Cat Bonds	Multi-ETFs	EM Debt

A large income is the best recipe for happiness I ever heard of.
—Jane Austen

Tired of earning nothing on your investments? That's only the second-best reason to look at alternatives for income.

The first is how dangerous the typical "safe" income sources have become. Bond funds have sopped up trillions of dollars over the past few years. No surprise; the very name purrs security. After all, a bond is the classic safe investment, and a fund provides diversity. Belt and suspenders, right? And all those investors have done very well, as interest rates kept moving to one historic low after another. All as comfy as an old pair of slippers.

With mousetraps inside. One fund, run by possibly the world's best—and certainly best-known—fixed income manager, dropped 30% in just five weeks in the fall of 2012. And that was without a big rate rise or major market crisis. If interest rates do lurch upward, the resulting fall in bond prices will resemble a Wile E. Coyote classic.

Inflation tremors that would spark interest rate increase have indeed been hard to sense, and the quietude has induced a sense of security in most investors. But just as the incredible pressures of tectonic plates muscling against one another can yield a silent and long-lasting draw, so can the awesome inflationary and deflationary forces now at war neutralize each other for an extended period.

But when slippage finally does occur, and one plate slides over the other, the landscape is profoundly altered in seconds. And that is a very real possible outcome of the financial forces standoff, too: we have been, and remain, at risk of both devastating deflation and runaway inflation.

Inflation is the more likely outcome, given the absolute resolution of the world's bankers, deeply schooled on the Great Depression, to avoid a repeat. And they've got the ultimate weapon, if they continue to use it: instant, electronic money creation from thin air, invoked by recitation of magic incantations such as "quantitative easing." Poof, money appears, no laborious lamp-rubbing required!

(In that, by the way, we have a macabre advantage over the infamous German hyperinflation of the '20s, which was hindered by its reliance on physical printing processes so that, eventually, new bills were printed on only one side so as to facilitate the inevitable reissuance process. Chalk one up for progress: our inflation technology has really improved.)

Whether anyone admits it or not, a key driver of the Fed's approach is indeed to inflate away the debt of both the government and the populace. Paying off our debts to China with less-valuable dollars is a way to make our national debt load more manageable; housing price inflation is the only short-term cure for the 20% of U.S. homes that are still worth less than the mortgages on them.

The belief is that a "controlled inflation" can be induced, and then tamed when necessary. Well, there's a first time for everything, I guess.

So the danger in bonds is easy to see. Inflation means higher interest rates; and those crush bond values. The real problem is that there's no offsetting reward: in this environment, you are not being paid adequately to take the interest rate risk inherent in these instruments. As Warren Buffett says: "Bonds promoted as offering risk-free returns are now priced to deliver return-free risk."

To get some perspective, this chart shows the number of years in which various levels of interest rates have prevailed.

TREASURY BOND INTEREST RATES SINCE 1900

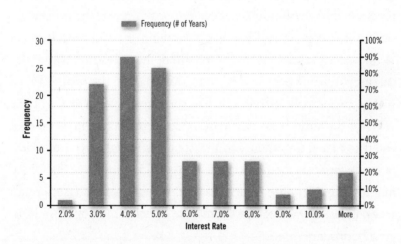

Source: Observations, http://observationsandnots.blogspot.com

See that tiny column way over there on the far left? That's us. Rates have been this low, in other words, less than 5% of the time since 1900. If they go back to, say, a very historically normal number like 5%, maybe 40% of the value of longer-term bonds bought today will be wiped out. That's what Mr. Buffett means.

This odd combination of all risk and no reward in traditional yield strategies makes finding intelligent income plays awfully difficult. The response of many investors is to take whatever interest rate the bond market is willing to give, knowing full well that if interest rates rise, the value of their bonds will fall. But they comfort themselves by thinking, Hey, if that happens, I'll just hold the bond to maturity and get my money back.

Well, it is true that even if bond prices plummet, you can hold them to maturity and have your principal repaid. *But the basic idea of a bond is to protect your purchasing power over time.* On that key mission, your investment will have failed. By definition, if inflation has accelerated and interest rates have risen, the dollars you get back at maturity will not be worth the same as the dollars you invested. They will purchase fewer goods. You will be poorer.

But not as poor as if you had invested in a bond fund instead. With very rare exceptions,* bond funds have no maturity; they don't return your principal at some given date in the future. What you get when you redeem is whatever your pro-rata share of the value of the fund is on that date . . . and if interest rates do rise, you'll get back less than you invested. As noted, given how low rates are right now, and how far they could easily rise, that "less" might easily turn into "much less" or perhaps even "a fraction of."

So please do not make the mistake of believing bond funds, or even bonds, are safe.

Instead we need reliable income with minimal exposure to rising rates. Several solid alternatives provide just that by offering

---

* A brand-new class of "bullet bond" funds do now plan to hold bonds to maturity and then distribute the proceeds.

yields that can rise over time . . . that may not totally nullify interest rate risk, but it sure takes some of the sting out. They also offer several other advantages: the rates are usually better than those of fixed income instruments; many also carry tax advantages; and some convey rights, not just in income streams, but also in underlying assets that themselves should increase in value during inflationary periods, a second level of protection.

Not a bad set of benefits, but also not complete. Naturally, a panoramic portfolio seeks income from different sectors and regions of the world's economies. And a key element of absolute diversification is to expand the number and types of obligors making payments into the portfolio, in order to limit simple credit risk. Sources like royalties and MLPs, where the ultimate payers are diverse groups of users, rather than a single corporate or governmental entity, serve that purpose nicely.

With all that in mind, here are eight places to look for inflation-protected income that should also reduce your portfolio's vulnerability to economic shocks.

MLPs

Master limited partnerships, MLPs, are a unique and very underappreciated asset class. Congress created these special vehicles back in the '80s to spur energy infrastructure construction, and you could almost say it went overboard bestowing investor incentives to kick-start that effort. But let's not look a gift horse in the mouth.

What's the special sauce? MLPs trade publicly, do not pay entity-level tax, pay out nearly all their net income directly to unit holders, and, here's the big one, can actively manage energy businesses to grow distributions. That last bit is really interesting, because the usual trade-off for exemption from entity-level taxation in publicly traded vehicles is that they must remain passive investors (think REITs and mutual funds). This unique capability of MLPs, to operate as a normal business, but remain tax free, allows them to generate higher revenues for investors over time.

The most interesting sort of MLP for most investors are those active in the "midstream" sector. These companies provide the pipelines, storage facilities, and other plumbing to move energy products around the country. As natural gas becomes a more important element of the nation's economy—and perhaps even a key export—it's hard to see that function getting anything other than more important. That should keep revenue growth cooking and help this group maintain its long history of increasing distributions by something like 5% to 10% per year.

At the same time, established midstream MLPs carry less credit risk than typical yield instruments because of how they make their money. Their equipment is usually used by several, often super credit-worthy entities (like the very biggest energy companies) . . . chances of these MLPs not getting paid are darn low.

The kicker is that the yields they generate for investors are significantly tax-favored because they are treated as a "return of capital." Therefore, in general, no tax is due on the income streams they throw off until the cumulative distributions exceed the invested amount (or upon the investor's sale of the MLP units). A 6% yield suddenly looks more like 8% or 9%.

As you would expect, MLPs historically outperform fixed income instruments in rising interest rate environments. Nonetheless, they do retain some short-term price risk if interest rates suddenly shoot up dramatically, as essentially all yield instruments do. MLPs fit nicely into the noncorrelated component of our risk-tolerant portfolio . . . for the record, they have a nice low beta of under one-half.

The annoying thing is that it's harder to figure out exactly how to buy MLPs than you'd like. They do trade on the exchanges, which is great, but instead of the typical tax reporting form, you'll receive a K-1. That's the form that partners in a partnership get each year (because that's what you are), which can be a bit messy, especially because you may need to file tax returns in the numerous states where the MLP operates. So, direct ownership of MLPs is more pleasant for those with accountants.

A much bigger drawback faces investors who buy MLP mutual funds. These do report income to investors on the more comfortable 1099, but there's a heavy price to pay. First, you're losing out on the tax-advantaged income stream because distributions from mutual funds don't count as "return of principal." Second, mutual funds can't hold more than 25% of their assets in MLPs (a silly rule that should be repealed). Sparing you the technical details, the impact is that the mutual fund is itself paying tax on the MLP proceeds before passing them along to investors, thereby forfeiting one of the core benefits of a mutual fund. The double tax haircut means a big reduction in yield as compared to owning the MLP units directly.

Similar considerations apply to ETFs that hold MLP interests: you get diversification but lose two levels of tax benefits and wind up with substantially diminished yield. Another route is "exchange traded notes," which are debt obligations of an issuer, usually a bank, that pays an interest rate pegged to the return on a basket of MLPs. Yet again, though, you'll make the trade of getting a tidy 1099 but lose the "return of principal" tax advantage, and you also have exposure to the credit risk of the obligor; lack of that single-obligor risk is another reason to invest in MLPs in the first place.

The final publicly traded option for MLP investment is a small group of exchange-traded closed-end funds that invest exclusively in MLPs. Mostly, these carry the same tax haircut as the open-end mutual fund variety but partially compensate for that by using leverage to juice the returns.

Accredited investors have better choices. One is registered privates that hold MLP interests; these pass through all the tax benefits, provide diversification, and may require initial investments of perhaps only $10,000. Finally, for those who want to invest substantially larger amounts (over $100,000), an attractive option is to establish a separately managed account with a registered investment advisory firm that specializes in MLPs. These should also give you access to the upstream (exploration and development) and downstream (processing plant) MLPs, which probably require more homework and a better knowledge of the energy industry than most individual investors possess.

There are a couple of key issues to be careful about. One is **incentive distribution rights** (IDRs), which are meant to incent the management team but can work against investors in the long run. A second is that a wave of new MLPs has been hitting the market, and these may not feature top-tier management teams . . . even if the entity is new, it should be run by a group with a strong operating history. But, in general, recurring payments from reliable operating companies that have stable and growing businesses is a wonderful antidote to overexposure to typical bonds.

Royalties

Pharmaceutical companies pay royalties to drug patent holders; radio stations pay royalties to song copyright owners; energy firms pay royalties to landowners when they take natural gas from a property. There are numerous kinds, but as a class royalties can offer solid income streams that increase over time with minimal credit risk: rather like MLPs, most often they are paid either by a large array of different users or by very large and creditworthy users, or both. And the effective yields are usually well above rates payable on typical credit instruments.

The most common way to invest here is through a "royalty trust." These are a bit like MLPs, in that they are also publicly traded and do not pay tax at the entity level, but they own, and pay out, royalty rights from mineral and mining properties. As a way to play commodities, they're fantastic, and they can offer extremely high yields—often over 10%.

Do be careful about the volatility of these revenue streams . . . as commodity prices bounce around, so does the income from a royalty trust (generally, a plus during inflation). Also note that, unlike MLPs, royalty trusts can't acquire more assets after they get going, so eventually their income streams will simply expire (and, to be clear, royalty trust investments aren't bonds; there is no principal to get back). So make sure to check how long income is projected to continue before investing.

Other kinds of royalties offer more predictable returns. For example, pharmaceutical royalties have become wildly popular among family office investors lately, for predictable reasons: the income streams are completely uncorrelated to corporate and municipal credits, and to the overall market. They can rise over time from increased use by an aging population, as well as general inflation, and they are typically backed by payment flows from lots of large, healthy companies.

The normal investment here is through private transactions, either via a partnership that owns these sorts of rights or through ownership of bonds backed by them. There are also a few publicly offered bonds out there that are backed by these payment streams. These are fixed income instruments, without inflation protection, but the yields are decent, and the diversification you get from having this category of obligor—Big Pharma companies with rock-solid balance sheets, profit margins, and cash flows—is still useful.

Music royalties are a fascinating new entrant on this scene. You probably knew that record companies get paid when their hit recording gets played somewhere. But did you know that there's a different copyright holder who's also getting paid at the same time? There is, and as a group they've cranked out amazingly steady profits while the recording business itself has suffered all sorts of turmoil.

The hidden winner is the music "publisher." This is a company that owns the rights to the musical work—the song's words and notes—who gets paid every time the tune is "performed" by anyone: streamed over Pandora, sung on Broadway, or used in a commercial. The publisher's rights are completely different from those in a specific sound recording of the song by a given performer.

That's why the biggest part of Michael Jackson's estate was not his own work but his rights to a large chunk of the Beatles library. Those great songs of the '60s, constantly rerecorded and reused, are still churning out many millions of dollars a year for the publishers who own them.

One way to invest in this world is through bonds backed by these royalty streams, the pioneering offering of which were called "Bowie Bonds"—yes, after Ziggy Stardust. If you're not a Rocket Man fan, you can also scoop up bonds where backup is sung by James Brown, the Isley Brothers, or Rod Stewart. (And in a very similar way, you can also buy bonds supported by libraries of TV and movies.)

A few privately placed funds invest in music rights, and these are very attractive for accredited investors. Aside from strong yields (somewhere around 10%), there are two other nice features. One is that, because the music library itself is depreciable, the regular income thrown off by the library can be largely shielded from current income taxation. Second, the owners of the rights can make them more valuable by "working the catalog": promoting the songs for use in movies or jingles, driving greater play on radio, and the like. That increases not only the income stream but also the residual value of the library upon eventual exit.

Trademarks, too, produce regular and recurring revenues so . . . why not? Yep, Bill Blass, Guess?, and even Sears have securitized their trademark revenue streams.

Today, the cutting edge of this space is right where you'd expect it to be: online. You can now purchase direct ownership of, or interests in, songs and other royalty-generating properties through Web-based exchanges. (See the resources pages for a couple.) Suddenly, eBay is looking a little dated.

Cat Bonds

Want a really uncorrelated income source? Try hurricanes.

No kidding. "Cat" (short for catastrophe) bonds are part of a rapidly growing set of insurance-related products, and they pay interest rates well above typical bonds. About $6 billion of dollar-denominated cat bonds issued in 2012 had yields of 9% percentage points more than short-term lending rates, fully 3% more than similar junk bonds . . . and with very little credit risk.

You can think of cat bonds as, essentially, reverse insurance policies. They are issued by property and casualty insurance companies looking to lay off the risk of a specific big catastrophe. Investors buy, say, a three-year hurricane bond and collect that fat coupon . . . so long as there aren't any storms that hit a defined area within the life of the bond. If a hurricane does hit and causes a specified amount of damage during that time, the payments are reduced, or stop altogether. (Well, you knew there had to be a catch.)

The losses are usually calculated with pre-agreed mathematical models to protect investors from questionable claims adjustments by the insurance company. And it's not an all-or-nothing bet, as damage has to exceed a specified amount for bondholder payments to suffer, rather like a deductible on your homeowner's policy.

These juicy returns and total noncorrelation with traditional financial markets make for a fascinating combination. The supply is not huge, but the durations are short, so new bonds do come to market frequently. And given the increasing frequency of severe weather events, it's almost a sure thing that this market will continue its rapid expansion.

(If you're interested in playing the global warming trend, by the way, take a look at **weather derivatives**. These don't fit into the income category, but for amateur meteorologists who enjoy taking a flyer, there's nothing quite like them.)

Expect more of these "ILS"—insurance-linked securities—in the future, as the capital markets take an ever increasing role in risk distribution, and insurance companies find better pricing in the capital markets than they can get from more traditional reinsurers. For example, some governments already issue bonds to protect themselves against excessive lottery payouts. And a big "life settlements" market has developed recently, which allows seniors to monetize their life insurance by selling them to hedge funds at a discount to their policy payoff. A little morbid, I guess, but the hedge funds do eventually collect.

Emerging Market Debt

There are many reasons that emerging market debt instruments bear so much higher rates of interest than U.S. obligations. Partly, it's the perceived safety of U.S. instruments, and partly, it's fear of inflation (as if that's not a problem here!). And then there's the currency risk that you're taking in those foreign jurisdictions. But it's very hard to ignore six or eight extra percentage points of interest these days.

Bonds of countries like Peru, Turkey, Venezuela, and Russia offer attractive yields, and probably less risk, than their high interest rates would seem to indicate.

Sara Zavos of Oppenheimer Funds makes a fantastic point about this category: "These are not your grandfather's emerging markets." What she means is that the traditional concern about emerging country debt has been inflation, but that this generation of emerging market central bankers and treasury officials are infinitely more sophisticated than their predecessors. Many have exactly the same education and outlook as our own top finance professionals: they were all classmates at Harvard and Yale. And most also have an easier time than the Fed dealing with the issue: they don't have a "dual mandate" under which job creation is one of their goals, and so can focus exclusively on monetary stability.

In addition, many countries offer much stronger protection and healthier regard for bondholders than they do for stockholders.

Some very sophisticated investors wouldn't touch Russian equities but love the bonds.

As these economies mature, it's highly likely that their "real" interest rates will come into line with those of the developed countries at some rate that's in between the two extremes one sees today. So, very big picture: there's a good chance that you can pick up both high nominal interest rates now and also capital appreciation in the future, as global interest rates converge over time.

Volatility in these instruments is a given, and a long-term view is definitely necessary. Because hedging out the currency risk is so expensive, the best idea is to accept it, and treat the currency exposure as another element of portfolio diversification. So the level of country-by-country investment must be carefully calibrated. This is one of those areas where active management is worth paying for: well-run mutual funds look a lot safer than passive ETFs here, and there are many good ones to choose from.

Especially as an alternative to the risky high-yield corporate bonds that have been booming of late, the benefits of well-chosen foreign debt look more interesting all the time: much greater income, long-term capital gain potential, and diversification.

Multiclass ETFs

One of the more interesting new entrants in the alternative income scene is "multiclass" ETFs, a sort of one-stop shop for diversified and uncorrelated income. They combine investments in categories like REITs, MLPs, royalties, and domestic and foreign high-dividend stocks. Obviously this is a very convenient way to get exposure to a diverse group of sources that should offer the prospect of higher income in inflationary periods. Many competing products are being rushed to market, so remember it's best to stick with large, well-known issuers when considering these new instruments.

And also remember to examine the total fees carefully . . . uncorrelated income is great only if you actually get it, and fees in these vehicles can definitely add up. Otherwise, the only significant fly in the ointment here is that, depending on exactly which ETF you acquire, the underlying instruments could overlap with other income sources in your portfolio and so create some concentration risk in specific asset classes.

Specialty Finance

Specialty finance offers some of the very best yield opportunities out there. The area includes asset-backed lending, equipment leasing, accounts receivable factoring, and a wide variety of consumer loans. In the past, banks would have been the providers of the credit facilities of this nature; but for various reasons, including regulatory limitations around the underlying business activity or regulatory capital requirements, a (very profitable) opportunity has been left open to hedge funds and other non-traditional lenders.

A fun example is slot machine finance. Very often, when you walk through a gaming floor, all those rows and rows of machines are not actually owned by the casino—they're leased. The real owners install the slots, run the wires back to their servers in the back room, and provide all the software necessary to operate the units and do the accounting. For that, the casinos pay over maybe 20% of the daily machine profits to the owners, who can typically recover their acquisition costs over a couple of years and then enjoy an ongoing cash stream for several more.

The returns are remarkably stable, especially away from the big resort destinations. For local casinos, the average "drop," the daily profit per machine, didn't budge from its $100 historical average in the recession (each day, they take in about $1,000 and pay back about $900). Slots produce income that essentially automatically adjusts for inflation, and they also have the simple advantage that they can be moved to better-performing locations if necessary.

Now, some would probably argue that an essentially identical idea is litigation finance, but we're not that cynical. Yep, there's a whole pile of capital providers out there providing the fuel to propel America's ferocious litigation engines. The focus is on highly complex cases, like class actions and patent prosecution. These lenders handicap the chances of the plaintiffs winning or the defendants settling, what the insurance coverage looks like, and the likely sizes of the awards, and then figure the price they can pay to buy into the claims. It works out surprisingly very well for many of the funds specializing in the space. So you can sleep well, knowing our armies of trial lawyers have job security.

On a much more mundane level, several groups specialize in classic factoring. One quite profitable activity is buying up the contracts under which furniture stores sell their sofas on a monthly payment plan. Obviously, the trick here is in understanding what the default patterns typically look like, and forecasting how much worse they might get in a recessionary period. The target list of receivables goes on and on, from dentists' bills to used-car loans. Properly bought, these sorts of loan portfolios can throw off very attractive income, but they are, of course, highly correlated to overall economic conditions . . . unlike MLPs, the obligors aren't exactly Exxon.

Unfortunately, it's tough for nonaccredited investors to find opportunities in this area. But for those who can buy private placements, many "ABL"—asset-backed lending—and credit hedge funds pursue these sorts of specialty finance deals, very often borrowing themselves to increase returns to investors. As a result, total yields can reach well into the upper teens. Obviously, those rates are hard to duplicate elsewhere.

Corporate Loans: Mezz Debt, BDCs, and Floaters

As just noted, banks are far less active lenders these days, but companies still need to borrow. That's created an awful lot of opportunities for investors outside the traditional, big corporate bond world. The allure is higher yields, shorter duration, and often floating rates that add a layer of inflation protection.

Mezz Debt

You'll recall the description in chapter 3 of how "LBO" transactions work . . . well, here's your chance to provide some of the "L," and you can get paid handsomely for it. Over the last several years, returns have been averaging in the low double digits, obviously tremendously more than most debt instruments.

Mezzanine debt is the unsecured debt component of those leveraged buyouts, so if things go badly, the loans are toast. But don't forget that in the typical LBO deal, some very smart, professional money is sitting at the bottom of the capital stack, in equity; and it will evaporate unless all the debt is repaid (and the sooner, the better). Having high-caliber investors sitting in a junior position provides an interesting endorsement—after all, they did their own analysis and apparently decided that the debt would all be paid.

The traditional way into a mezz debt fund is through a private partnership, of which there are many. The usual suspects—KKR, Goldman, Carlyle, Blackstone, and Oaktree—run the largest ones. As you know, these will typically require significant management fees, but especially given the extra yield versus the credit risk issue, paying a manager is worthwhile. A couple of newer mutual funds and closed-end funds also specialize in these instruments, and you can expect to see more as many of the largest PE firms turn to retail markets for a bigger pool of capital to fund their deals.

BDCs

A "business development company" is a publicly traded, nontaxable entity that invests in middle-market and smaller companies. A few make equity investments, but most are lenders, and these tend to provide a fairly high coupon income stream backed by a diverse pool of companies from around the country.

In some ways, BDCs are like junior varsity PE shops, so it's not surprising that several are managed by the biggest private equity names, like Apollo, BlackRock, and KKR. These sponsors should certainly know a good credit from a bad one. And exchange-traded BDCs are, naturally, extremely liquid. Especially for nonaccredited investors, they're not a bad way into the world of direct corporate finance.

A downside of BDC investing is that this is a pretty "correlated" asset class: if the economy tanks, these will get hit, just as they did (badly) in 2008. On the other hand, they do have a very diverse set of obligors and can ride out an increase in interest rates because the new loans they make will always be at market rates.

And if the economy really does start to pick up steam, BDCs might do well because of the way banks have exited the middle-market lending world . . . they'll have an expanded list of attractive deals to do.

Traded BDCs are easy to find, research (definitely recommended! the quality level is all over the map), and buy. Note: there are also many nontraded BDCs out there, but those make the "red flag" list in chapter 10.

Floaters

Floaters are corporate loans in which the interest rates are pegged to a benchmark, and reset periodically, so they track overall market rates. They're also called leveraged loans, which sounds about as redundant as you can get, but the name is meant to imply that they're issued by companies that already have a lot of debt outstanding (rather like mezz debt). Almost by definition, then, they carry higher credit risk than traditional bonds, but they compensate for that with meaningfully higher rates and, even better, inflation protection via the interest reset feature. Very generally, the yields are comparable to junk bonds, but that reset mechanism makes them much safer from interest-rate risk.

You can't buy these directly. They're purely "over the counter"–type instruments, and it can take weeks to find a buyer for a given instrument. In addition, they can require care and feeding—for example, holders are often asked to agree to some changes in the underlying terms (aka "covenants"). Therefore, they have largely been the provenance of institutional buyers until recently. But, as with so many alternatives, normal investors have recently gained good options for participating. A growing number of mutual funds specialize in the space; and in the latest twist, several so-called actively managed ETFs have hit the market (to a great response).

Peer-to-Peer Lending

If you want to see the future of personal finance, check out the big peer-to-peer lending sites like LendingClub.com and Prosper .com. While you're at it, you can pick up high-yield bond-type returns from a completely different class of borrowers, and with much less **duration risk** to boot (that is, their value won't fall too much in a rising-rate environment).

The concept has been around for many years but has recently passed the credibility threshold: use technology to facilitate transactions between people with money to lend on one side, and individuals who need to borrow on the other. Countless consumers with reasonable credit scores are stuck with extremely high rates on credit card debt and would be thrilled to take out a consolidation loan at a lower rate. Countless investors are desperate for yield and can stomach a little risk. Peer-to-peer lending brings them together.

The sites that run these operations perform the necessary middleman functions at a fraction of a bank's overhead (or hassle). Borrowers fill out a very simple loan request and provide their credit scores and employment status, along with a short explanation of why they're good candidates for a loan. The sites verify the data and segment the lenders into different risk categories who pay accordingly different rates.

Usually, however, no one lender fills a given loan request; investor dollars are spread across many borrowers (radically reducing risk), and borrowers effectively borrow from a given consortium of lenders. Naturally, some defaults are fully expected and are factored in to anticipated returns to investors; and the sites do provide collection services. More important, so far payment experience has been more or less in line with charge off expectations, given the borrowers' histories and credit ratings. That is: lenders have netted very nice returns.

Peer-to-peer lending is a classic example of using technology to eliminate middlemen and create new value for both sides, and the party doing the disintermediation: the sites charge origination and servicing fees to turn profits but add far less drag than traditional banks. Almost any investor can participate, and the returns can run to the low teens for the riskier borrowers—even within this category, the expected charge off rates have been in line with projections.

The loans are short term (one, three, or five years) and fully amortizing—the balance is paid during the loan life, not in one slug at the end, as is true with most bonds. That's one reason why they carry fairly minimal duration risk. This is a key point: as we've noted, the market is simply not rewarding investors for duration risk right now; but you can get paid to take a little credit risk, which is exactly the trade-off involved here. To get a toe in the water, investors can start with small amounts spread across a diverse group of borrowers with better credit ratings.

In a somewhat similar vein, but for sophisticated investors only, is the rise of "micro PE." This is a "roll your own" approach to private equity loans into small and midmarket firms, which use the proceeds for acquisitions, expansion, and restructuring. Several high-quality "private placement platforms" provide the opportunity to identify, and then perform due diligence on, these would-be corporate borrowers. The transactions are not for neophytes, but smaller institutions, family offices, and very high-net-worth individuals may find opportunities to lend on a fully secured basis at rates many hundreds of points above LIBOR.

NOT-SO-ALTERNATIVE INCOME SOURCES

For sake of completeness, we'll also briefly describe three income opportunities that are somewhere between "traditional" and "alternative." These are not really our focus, but since everyone's hungry for yield, we'd hate to leave them out.

REITs

I'm sure you know about REITs, real estate investment trusts. They are passive vehicles that collect rents and mortgage payments from every part of the real estate world: residential and commercial, with subcategories like health care, luxury resorts, shopping malls, or even self-storage.

REIT dividend rates usually run way ahead of bond yields and are clearly worth a look. But they have lately been highly correlated to financial equities, so be careful about thinking they provide great diversification benefits. More generally, many have not performed well recently, partially a consequence of too few enormous players chasing too few properties (and hence overpaying for them). There are other issues, too, including that some are actually borrowing to cover current distributions—obviously unhealthy in the long run. REITS can't actually buy and develop properties (as can **REOCs**); and they are often caught with very long-term leases that can't be adjusted in times of inflation. So, good yields notwithstanding, be a touch careful with these.

High-Yield Bonds

High-yield bonds obviously are still bonds, and so share the concerns mentioned above. However, they do offer great yields that would take some sting out of a fall in prices, and they tend to do well in periods when the public equity markets tread water. They actually did somewhat better than stocks in the crash.

However, the market looks dangerously bubbly as this is written. During 2012 more high-yield bonds were issued than during the previous three years combined, and more than twice as much as the previous record. The credit quality investors are willing to accept keeps falling, clearly indicated by the market's ability to absorb **PIK bonds**.

So: be very, very careful. If the yields are just too much for you to pass up, this is another area in which a mutual fund or an actively managed ETF—or even a separate account with a firm specializing in the asset class—may be the best choice because the higher fees are partially covered by the bond yields, and professional managers (and diversification) could make a very big difference in long-term performance.

High-Dividend and Preferred Stocks

High-dividend stocks—whether common or preferred—tend to outperform most other assets in periods of low or no economic growth (which might feel familiar in the current market).

Common stocks, of course, can absorb inflation much better than traditional fixed income assets. They are, however, very obviously subject to serious tumbles in adverse economic periods and, like high-yield bonds, have generally become somewhat expensive as everyone hunts for yield plays. The biggest trick is picking companies that increase dividends over time . . . so once again, a good manager is important and is probably worth the fees. Mutual funds and separately managed accounts are most likely the best bets.

Preferred stocks are very popular choices among Registered Investment Advisors looking to add yield to client portfolios. The benefit is that the dividend is promised (unlike common stock dividends, which can be halted at any time by the issuer), and the yields are generally north of choices with comparable credit risk. The downside is these are more subject to inflation risk, since, unlike common stocks, holders do not usually participate in the upside if the company's value increases.

In Review

MLP investments and various kinds of royalty streams are terrific sources of noncorrelated income, and also offer rising income to help offset the risks of inflation. Be careful exactly how you buy, as the net after-tax yields from different vehicles can vary dramatically.

In the search for yield, emerging market debt is one of the better choices; the many extra points of interest income just cannot be ignored. But invest behind a good active manager.

Multiclass ETFs are a strong new yield choice for average investors, combining income flows from various other sources mentioned in this chapter.

In the current market, it is difficult to get compensated for taking duration risk, so take as little as possible. It is easier to get paid to assume credit risk, which, in small doses, might make that a good idea . . . in this regard, while peer-to-peer lending is new, it is also an extremely interesting option.

For similar reasons, consider floater funds and BDCs, which offer publicly traded access to corporate loans with higher yields than traditional fixed income investments.

For accredited investors, mezz debt funds, specialty finance, and royalty partnerships can add hundreds of basis points of current yield. Another way to do that, without dipping into lower-credit-quality issuers, is to take on a small insurance role with cat bonds—seems unusual, perhaps, but, again, at least you're getting paid for the risks you're taking.

The more usual suspects for higher current income—REITs, high-yield bonds, and high-dividend common and preferred stocks—are just that, usual. As a result, they are often overbid; the numerous alternatives described in this chapter may provide better risk/return characteristics and better protection against inflation along with their powerful noncorrelation benefits.

Final Thought

Despite all the talk about the desperate search for yield, it is not so terribly difficult to get higher income and inflation protection. You just can't rely on traditional investments to do it.

CHAPTER 6

Broadening the Base for Risk Reduction (Job 2)

Long/Short	Arbitrage	Funds of Funds	Farmland
Managed Futures	Black Swan	Global Blue Chips	Inefficient Markets

The essence of investment management is the management of risks, not the management of returns.

—BENJAMIN GRAHAM

Over the past four hundred years, the world has endured a significant financial crisis, on average, once a decade. You might have noticed that the pace of events isn't exactly slowing down.

We already know that loss avoidance is the biggest single factor in accumulating long-term wealth. That's gotten tougher, because the world's ever greater complexity means ever greater instability. But it's also gotten easier, because the ways in which we can diversify and manage risk have also multiplied.

Good thing, because diversifying with different U.S. stocks is like creating a balanced diet from different brands of breakfast cereals. Of course, U.S. stocks will remain a staple for most investors, an excellent source of longer-term gains . . . nonetheless, in the typical long-only format, they are overemphasized.

This chapter therefore focuses on adding active risk management to limit losses in stock downturns and, crucially, adding several sources of uncorrelated returns. Just as football players widen their stances to prepare for a hit, portfolios should have a broad base to better absorb blows . . . that's a big step toward making them "risk-tolerant."

Given the pivotal status of equities for average investors—and the ongoing risks of major market reversals—we'll kick off this chapter with what may be the one change that would make the most difference for the most people: modifying a long-only stock approach to include some long/short strategies.

Here's a nice graphical representation of why adding this kind of approach can be so important to your long-term wealth. The lighter areas show major stock market declines; the darker areas display the performance of long/short strategies during those periods.

WORST DRAWDOWN: LONG/SHORT EQUITY VERSUS U.S. STOCKS, JANUARY 1990–DECEMBER 2011

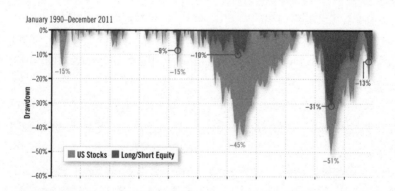

Source: Altergris

We've beaten endlessly on the "lose less, have more" theme, so we won't say anything further on that. Oh, OK, maybe we will. Here's the companion chart that shows how much better investors in this strategy have fared, as compared to long-only investors:

INDEX COMPARISON: LONG/SHORT EQUITY VERSUS U.S. STOCKS: VALUE OF AN INITIAL $1,000 INVESTMENT, JANUARY 1990–DECEMBER 2011

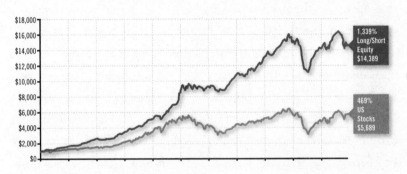

Source: Altegris

So how does a good long/short fund both make money and limit downside risk? Here's a very profitable real-world example.

A technology-focused long/short manager thought Seagate's hard drive business would carry the stock higher as the overall markets improved in late 2011. Its bitter competitor, Western Digital, would be the obvious offsetting short, but a ho-hum trade suddenly became a big bet when he looked at some weather maps. Horrible flooding was projected in Thailand, where both companies had major facilities . . . but Seagate's were on much higher ground. Perfect: he went long Seagate and shorted Western Digital. Sure enough, as the tech market rose, so did the flood tide; 75% of Western Digital's production was halted, while

Seagate's was barely impacted. As the stock market digested the news over a couple of weeks, the stocks moved in opposite directions. A double win with very little risk.

Thus, the best long/short managers make money "on both sides of the book," on both their longs and their shorts. They construct their portfolios so that the sides of the pair are similar enough that they hedge each other but also have a chance to produce profits from asymmetrical behavior. Watch out for funds that advertise themselves as long/short but actually get the short exposure through index puts or other broad-based derivatives. Those are giving up half their chances to make money.

One other point to understand is "net exposure." If you've got $100 on a long position and $100 on a short position, your net exposure to the market's overall direction is zero, as it was in that early Ford/GM example. You're "market neutral." But most long/short managers actually have a "bias" and are either overall positive or negative on the market . . . they'll make more if they're right, but they're still partially hedged if they're wrong. For example, one who thinks that the S&P is headed up might have 80% of the fund in long positions, and 20% of it in short positions. That would give his fund a "net long exposure" of 60%: 80 minus 20.

And if the fund uses leverage, which most of them do, the fund could have a "gross exposure" of well more than 100%: it might be 120% long and 60% short, and so have a gross exposure of 180% while being net long 60%.

The key point: a manager who runs a low net exposure (say 20%) and a gross exposure of 100% or less (that is, he doesn't use leverage) isn't taking much market risk. If he is also stamping out gains consistently, you've probably just discovered real alpha. That takes skill.

OK, that's how the strategy works. Now: how should you invest in it? This is an area in which liquid alternatives can be extremely attractive, the prototypical "smart beta" investments. Many long/short mutual funds do the necessary and carry relatively low fees. Now, you're unlikely to get that alpha-generating, low net exposure guy in a mutual fund—for him, it's probably a 2 and 20 old-school private placement deal—but for getting risk-managed exposure to equities, these funds are tough to beat.

The obvious and easy option is a mutual fund that runs the strategy with its internal money managers. But don't forget that exactly which funds you choose matters hugely. Recently, many famous mutual fund brand names have leapt into the strategy with unproven internal managers. No need to go there, as several established funds have performed admirably over the past several years.

A newer approach is a "mutual fund of funds," in which the mutual fund allocates to several outside L/S managers. Those can be other mutual funds or true hedge fund managers who become subadvisors to the mutual fund's assets. This gets you both active risk management and a combination of slightly different long/short styles, all in a single, liquid investment. As a general approach to getting active risk management into an equity portfolio, these sorts of funds make a pretty compelling argument.

On the other hand, be wary of the so-called 130/30 funds, which are often marketed as long/short strategies. Well, sort of. These sell short 30% of their portfolio, take the cash, and invest it in more longs. Thus, their gross exposure is 160%, and they are actually 100% net long, which makes these more of a bet on manager skill than is a principled way to get risk-adjusted equity exposure. The track records have been disappointing.

Finally, there are the formulaic "replication" funds and ETFs, which, as it sounds, attempt to mimic the performance of real long/short hedge funds. Some do that by reviewing SEC filings of hedge funds to see which stocks they have been buying and selling, and then do the same. Some use algorithms to look backward at that darn average hedge fund performance to find investing formulas that would have replicated those numbers. Either way, the whole methodology is backward-looking, and there's something fundamentally perverse about practicing active risk management by looking in the rearview mirror.

Other Relative Value Equity Strategies

Several arbitrage strategies can do very well in most sorts of market environments and are also excellent ways to diversify away from long-only strategies.

Convertible arbitrage is the true classic, a style that performed spectacularly for many years leading up to the crash: up about 100% from 2000 to '08, with close to double-digit returns each year. And it's done very well since then, too. But . . . things were downright ugly in the crash. That history is instructive.

A $10,000 convertible bond gives the bondholder the right, but not the obligation, to convert his bond into a given number of shares of stock of the issuer. That's a wonderful option to have in the case of rising rates, where the stock should do relatively better than the bonds; and, independently of interest rates, the ability to convert into common stock provides upside should the company go on a tear. For that reason, old-fashioned, long-only convertible bond funds are an extremely reasonable place to invest for inflation-protected income, and they were excluded from the previous chapter only because they aren't "alt" enough.

Anyway, as you can easily guess, that option to convert has real value. It is exactly like owning a separate option to buy the stock with the proceeds of the bond sale. And options to buy most companies' stocks trade in the market. But the prices of the two options—the one that's truly separate and traded on an exchange, and the one that's embedded in the convertible bond—are sometimes out of sync with each other. Arbitrage time!

There are several ways to profit from the assumption that, over time, those two prices will come into line, and the resulting bet involves very little risk and small but steady returns.*

So managers typically add leverage to get those returns up to attractive levels. In normal markets, whether up or down, that all works very well indeed, which is why the strategy did so well for so long.

But in 2008 all hell broke loose. Convertible arb went from being one of the very best-performing strategies to the absolute worst. Two impossible-to-foresee factors converged. First, some of the biggest holders of convertibles, like Freddie, Fannie, and Lehman, all failed simultaneously and were forced to dump all their convertible bonds at once. Second, emergency rules limited the ability to short stocks, a critical element of a convertible arbitrage strategy, meaning no new buyers would step in. Leverage, and margin calls, left a desolate landscape of smoking ruins.

(Here, by the way, is an ideal example of why backward-looking mathematical models overstate the safety of a specific strategy: they can never account for never-before-seen events like new limits on short selling.)

---

* The basic trick is to buy the convertible bond and sell the underlying stock in a way that makes the fund neutral to overall stock market moves, or **delta neutral**. In the meantime, the fund is capturing the income from the bond and the short sale proceeds.

In some ways, convertible arbitrage strategies are a poster child for a panoramic portfolio. They're investible for the simple reason that they tend to do very well in most environments . . . you don't want to ignore them just because they depend on some degree of regular market behavior. On the other hand, you'll want some strategies in the portfolio that should perform well when this one doesn't.

Merger arbitrage and **statistical (stat) arbitrage** strategies have similar attributes. When markets are functioning normally, and the rules of the game don't get changed in the middle, they're pretty reliable ways to broaden your investing horizon.

Like long/short strategies, these arbitrage approaches can be accessed through mutual funds that you can easily locate through the Morningstar or your broker's Web site. But with these strategies, too, the difference between the best-performing managers and the rest of the crowd is pretty substantial . . . and the very best of all, as usual, are most often found in a 2 and 20, private-placement structure.

A note here on one related strategy that might be too risky for typical investors: credit arbitrage. These funds exploit microscopic differences in credit instruments, often esoteric derivatives, and then multiply them with healthy doses of debt steroids. When, in the last crisis, credit prices moved in unexpected directions, margin calls issued, and access to leverage was withdrawn at the same time, many players in the space were crushed. It's often said that funds pursing credit arbitrage are "picking up nickels in front of steamrollers."

Hedged Strategy Mixers

Earlier we talked about mutual funds that invest in long/short strategies by allocating out to other managers. That's one example of a "fund of funds," a common idea in alternative investing: one fund invests in several others. Sometimes, as with the long/short mutual funds, the idea is to diversify across managers running the same strategy. But sometimes the idea is to mix it up with different strategies, aggregating many styles into one product. Many liquid alternatives and privately placed partnerships follow each route, so there's no shortage to choose from.

"Multi-alternative" mutual funds offer this sort of one-stop shopping: they invest in a broad set of underlying strategies, including currencies, managed futures, and several kinds of arbitrage styles. Obviously, that sounds great, and it can be. But make sure you're getting the noncorrelated returns you're paying for. How? Well, you'll recall that beta is a measure of how closely a fund mimics the movement of the general market. The marketing materials for the fund will show you it's beta, and you want to see a score of .7 or less (and less is better here). As the beta approaches 1, it indicates the fund matches ever more closely the movement of the overall market . . . and thus that it may not be worth the extra fees these vehicles typically charge.

Privately placed funds of funds, for accredited investors only, can be even better diversifiers *if* you can get the right kind at the right price, mostly because, freed from mutual fund constraints, they have many more ways to invest.

These classic "FoFs" became very popular after 2000. The original rationale was to allow merely affluent investors to gain access to the really fancy hedge fund managers who demanded minimum investments of $10 million or more. FoFs aggregated lots of "small" $2 million and $3 million checks so that, cumulatively, they would have enough to enter elite company. Though designed to provide access in this way, the structure provided a different benefit. If the FoF raised $2 million each from fifty investors, it could then make ten of those $10 million investments into different funds. FoFs quickly realized the benefits of marketing themselves for diversification, and many then ran wild with this rationale. Some funds offered access to many dozens, and oftentimes even hundreds, of managers.

Meanwhile, the all-too-apt joke became that "FoF" actually stood for "fund of fees." A typical FoF manager charged 1% management fee and a 10% success fee—but, of course, since he was usually investing in hedge funds with a 2 and 20 structure, the fees to the investor totaled 3 and 30. The defense was that: (1) diversification is important; and (2) the FoF managers were doing lots of necessary and difficult work in vetting and selecting the underlying funds, work nonexperts could not do well. That message resonated for a good while, and FoFs became absolutely enormous. Then came the crisis, and some big disappointments.

Their "sprinkler" diversification didn't work so well because there was far too little knowledge, or thinking, about how the various strategies would perform in a market crisis. (Recall that traditional hedge funds don't report their investment positions to anyone, including their investors.) Many slightly different equity-based hedged strategies, classified into different buckets and so presented as diverse, were actually all completely vulnerable to the same risks. There was insufficient attention paid to real noncorrelation and absolute diversification: too many convergent strategies and not enough divergent ones. Even more to the point, several academic studies have now shown that once you get above about twenty-five underlying managers, a fund of funds starts to lose the benefits of diversification in any event . . . it becomes ever more a "beta" product.

Thus, the state-of-the-art thinking is that midsize FoFs, with a stable of twelve to twenty-five managers, work best. Funds of funds of this stripe—with a well-thought-through diversification strategy and well-chosen underlying managers—are very solid ways to reduce risk with a single investment.

The most compelling are FoFs that provide access to otherwise unreachable managers (their original purpose, after all). Some operate in emerging economies—say China—where doing the diligence and selecting fund managers on your own could prove just a bit challenging, even if your Mandarin is awesome. Some focus on capacity-constrained niche strategies, where alpha is much more achievable than in widely practiced strategies. And, as you'll see in the next chapter, FoFs with access to top venture capital and private equity funds may be the best way to approach those investment classes

Always, though, the big issue is simple: how's the performance after all the fees? And on that score there's some good news. Many newer-vintage FoFs have lower total fees and/or have adopted hurdles so that the manager doesn't get paid until after the investor has first earned a given return. And the very latest trend is toward registered privates, the baby bear structure of chapter 4; aside from the additional investor protections, these often carry lower fees as well. (Once again, check out the resources for help locating these.)

Farmland and Timber

OK, that timber part is, as they say in TV land, a tease. That wonderfully unique asset, really the only one that can perform all four of the investment jobs at once, belongs here too, but is actually described in chapter 8. You can flip forward now and check it out—especially the "TREITs" part—for it is one heck of a risk-reducer.

Meanwhile, let's talk about its sister asset class: farmland. The big argument for it is easy to guess: the demand for food will continue to skyrocket as frontier and developing economies progress, and as rising middle classes of the Arab Spring demand better and more reliable sources of protein. By one measure, if every person in China ate two extra eggs a week, it would require all the grain Canada currently produces just to feed the chickens. And, food aside, farmland is also in demand for biofuel production. Happily, North America has some of the world's most reliable land and its top expertise.

Annual returns from farmland have been very strong in the past few years, somewhere in the midteens when you include cash rents, profit-sharing income, and appreciation. The inflation benefits are obvious, for both the annual income stream and, more importantly, the residual value. That leads some people to call farmland "gold with a coupon." (Even through the horrendous drought of 2012, Midwest farms generated excellent returns, partly thanks to crop insurance.)

The bad news here is that there's already been a big move in farmland prices, especially for the best located: prime Iowa acreage may be in a bubble, with prices for ultra prime areas reaching records of $20,000 per acre in late 2012. On the other hand, the worldwide ratio of arable land per person keeps dropping, from almost three acres per person in 1960 to about one now, while demand for its output is nearly certain to rise. Obviously one wants to shop carefully, but this may be the sort of asset that doesn't require bargain hunting.

Publicly traded options are almost nonexistent, for the ETFs with "farm" in the title really include large agribusinesses, not at all the same thing. There are, however, many fine, midsized private partnerships in both the United States and Canada that provide expert land selection, management, and diversification. In fact, several of these are more "retail friendly" than other kinds of private partnerships, with lockups as short as three years and modest minimums.

Of course, direct ownership is always an option, but watch a few episodes of *Green Acres* first. You might conclude that using a good farm management company is the way to go. These will help you locate properties for purchase, arrange for tenant farmers to work them, and handle all the financial details like managing the profit sharing and crop insurance. That might just make direct ownership plausible.

Managed Futures

"Managed futures" investing is beginning to attract mainstream attention, and, as we mentioned back in chapter 4, that's for one good reason: it has shown excellent countercyclical tendencies in past stock market downturns. You can see that here:

CORRELATION TABLE, JANUARY 1997–MARCH 2012

	Managed Futures	Global Macro	Long/Short Equity	US Stocks	US Bonds
Managed Futures	1.00	0.52	-0.01	-0.16	0.24
Global Macro	0.52	1.00	0.72	0.45	0.17
Long/Short Equity	-0.01	0.72	1.00	0.76	-0.02
US Stocks	-0.16	0.45	0.76	1.00	-0.03
US Bonds	0.24	0.17	-0.02	-0.03	1.00

Source: Altegris

We've also already touched on the incredibly broad array of assets covered by managed futures, also that various long, short, volatility, and spread trading tactics are used. Therefore, average performance can be misleading: managed futures are no more a single asset class than hedge funds. And also like hedge funds, the best managers wildly outperform the worst ones.

Try to get to an industry cocktail party just to hear the chatter: "the thrust phase in gasoline is slowing," "lean hogs are in consolidation," or "a major seasonal top is due in lead." And that's before someone riffs on the latest correlation trends, like how the British pound will do as pork bellies rise. That's the talk, because of that "trend following" approach discussed earlier: mostly, these managers (or their computers) identify patterns between and among asset prices and then trade on the assumption that the trend will continue for a while. There is almost no fundamental analysis going on, quite probably one reason why the noncorrelation with the stock market is so strong.

In any event, the Morningstar MSCI Systematic Trading Hedge Fund Index has generated returns greater than the total returns of the S&P 500 since 1996, a pretty good reason all by itself to consider this category.

So how does one invest in "managed futures"? Traditionally, investors have signed up with a "CTA," a commodities trading advisor . . . which is a confusingly poor name for the guy. It sounds as though he should be someone like a traditional financial advisor, but that's not the case.

The CTA is not there to advise you, or develop a strategy around your needs or outlook; instead, when you invest in a CTA, you're buying into his preexisting trading strategy. In that sense, investing with a CTA is more like investing in a mutual fund with a very specific investing strategy. Therefore you should always insist on seeing his audited performance records. Audits are performed by the National Futures Association, which reviews each account type and determines return on investment net of all fees (which may sound familiar: 2 and 20 is common).

To get optimal diversification, wealthier investors will consider investing with four or five different CTAs, each with its own strategy. Unfortunately, that does take some money, because the minimums for well-established managers can easily reach a few hundred thousand dollars. Some first-timers therefore go through a pool run by a "CPO," a commodities pool operator, which is like a fund of funds for CTAs, with, as you'd expect, additional fee layers. There are also older-style funds sold through brokerage networks, but those tend to be very fee-heavy and nontransparent.

The best approach for many investors will be another of the new liquid alternatives, in this case mutual funds that invest in a group of managed futures managers. These essentially provide double diversification, into new kinds of strategies and different managers as well, and have generally performed their noncorrelated duties well since coming to market over the past couple of years.

Before you go hunting for these, there is one really critical distinction to understand. Some managed futures mutual funds (and ETFs) are passively managed, tracking an index, while others are actively managed. There's good historical evidence that the active variety outperforms the passive variety by a large margin. Once you see how these things work, that's totally unsurprising.

With managed futures, the "index" to which the ETFs and passively managed mutual funds are tied is the Diversified Trends Indicator (or a similar standard). But the DTI is not a normal index that simply aggregates prices on securities. It requires buying and selling asset classes as they move above or below long-term moving averages. Thus these funds are actually following an extremely basic, and static, trading model . . . one that is very easily gamed by smart traders on the other side, who know exactly what the model will tell large numbers of fund managers to do under certain circumstances. It's a clay pigeon at the Hedge Fund Manager Shooting Range.

So actively managed mutual funds specializing in managed futures strategies are the way to go for most investors. Some of these, like good funds of funds, aggregate the top CTAs and, in the latest twist, also use leading fixed income managers to oversee the dollars held aside to meet margin calls. But do be mindful of the fees, which can add up . . . even noncorrelation is worth only so much.

A NOTE ON CURRENCIES AND COMMODITIES

Some may wonder why there is no specific entry in this chapter on currencies or commodities. Both can indeed serve to diversify portfolios and reduce risks, and both are available in liquid and low-cost forms through ETFs and mutual funds. But to me these are probably too narrow to justify separate investment. Both can and will be utilized by CTAs, global macro, and other investment managers as tools, but having a permanent allocation to these classes can introduce some profound volatility to a portfolio that might outweigh their diversification benefits. Of course, if you do find that totally incredible manager whose track record just glimmers, and who has demonstrated low volatility with these assets, you'll get no argument here.

Uncorrelated Niche Strategies

Here's a group of strategies that do not mimic the general actions of the stock and bond markets at all. One manager of a top fund of funds in this space says, perfectly seriously, that he doesn't think about the stock market for more than ten minutes a year.

"Motivational arbitrage" is a common theme in this category. Some kinds of markets are dominated by very large participants for which minor price differences are simply not as important as other factors. One example, previously mentioned, is electricity trading; the utilities that buy are more driven by fear of brownouts than they are concerned with paying a bit more than absolutely necessary (especially because those costs flow through to their consumers, anyway). Carbon credit trading is similar, and quite inefficient in these, its early days. But even in well-developed, highly liquid markets, motivational arbitrage opportunities exist. Consider currencies.

You might well have thought of currency traders as extraordinarily price sensitive, given that microscopic moves in comparative rates often attract major press attention . . . and there's even a word, *pip*, for one one-hundredth of one percent, the increment in which those moves are measured. Nonetheless, some buyers and sellers are not so rigorous. Imagine a huge international conglomerate that has to convert hundreds of millions of foreign revenues into U.S. dollars in a short period before a quarter ends. It's whale eating plankton; in the sloppy process, pilot fish can live a good life. Of course the big company does care about the rate it gets, but it doesn't have the time, trading staff, or motivation to exact every pip. The professional traders on the other side live for such opportunities.

But of the niche strategies, my favorite has to be the funds that have made a fortune shorting Chinese stocks after a "reverse IPO."

To which you might well say: huh? But here goes. To get a stock listed on a U.S. exchange is pretty hard. You've got to file reams of papers, the SEC combs through all your details, and the underwriters, along with management, have liability if things aren't represented to the investing public accurately. There are lots of people and processes that help ensure all the closeted skeletons get outed.

But, in video game language, there's a cheat, a shortcut called a reverse IPO. It works because lots of public companies do very badly for a very long time and slowly become an empty shell . . . nobody cares about them, they don't conduct business, they have a bit of cash on the balance sheet, and they just linger, a corporate vegetable. They don't have much, but they do have a public listing.

A reverse IPO, also called a reverse takeover or reverse merger, happens when a private company merges with that dormant public company. The private company shareholders wind up with most of the postdeal stock, and its management takes over the combined operation. Prest-o Change-o,* your private company is now public.

Many Chinese firms used this shortcut simply to get the prestige of a public listing in the U.S., and some wanted to do legitimate secondary offerings. But I'm afraid that an unpleasantly high number of those reverse IPOs were very successful shams . . . after all, "China" and "incredible growth" are synonyms, right?

Sensing something was wrong with the amazing successes the companies reported, a few clever fund managers turned the

---

* For trivia fans: this was the title of a Bugs Bunny cartoon when the characters were in prototype; Bugs was a puppet in a magician's chest.

tables. They employed on-the-ground intelligence operations in China to discover, for example, that photos of gleaming corporate headquarters were listed at addresses of empty lots. Yep, it turned out that many, most famously Sino-Forest, were outright frauds. So the managers would short those companies' shares . . . and then publicly announce their findings. Boom! The stock would *Hindenburg*, and the funds made a fortune.

Yet another niche strategy might be filed under "if you can't beat 'em, join 'em": high-frequency trading. Here, the arbitrage is sheer speed; HFT firms quite literally compete with one another for advantages of nanoseconds—*billionths of a second*—in getting and sending data. There are many ways to shave time off trades: better bandwidth, more efficient algorithms, faster servers. But one incredibly simple way is to just pay up. The exchanges will happily rent you colocation space at a very healthy price, and each foot closer you are to their computers saves one of those precious nanoseconds. Here's one example of how that translates into reliable, if unspectacular, returns.

An "index arbitrage" takes advantage of the fact that ETFs hold static collections of securities. Especially amid high market volatility, the prices of the shares of an ETF will get slightly out of whack with the total value of the basket of securities it holds. Say an ETF that invests in the S&P index has a hundred million shares outstanding at a price of $10 a share, properly reflecting that the stocks it owns are indeed worth $1 billion at that moment. An order imbalance momentarily pushes the ETF price to $10.01 without any movement in the underlying stocks. Suddenly, there's a million dollars on the table. The HFTs light up, instantly selling the ETF and buying the right amount of every stock of the S&P index. You can see how it's simply a race to that million bucks . . . the first kid in the pool wins. And that's why so much is spent on hardware, software, efficient algorithms, and bandwidth.*

These sorts of niche strategies are gems of diversification: none of them track to how the overall financial markets are performing (but note that the more volatile those markets, the more opportunities for HFT shops). They can be tough to find, but several hedge and financial technologies ("fin tech") funds specialize in them, as do several funds of funds. (Also see the resources pages.)

Emerging Markets

It's almost necessary to have some exposure to the portions of the world that actually are growing. And some are on fire. Latin America has added more citizens to its middle classes over just two years than Texas has residents. Mexico, despite all its bad press, is a rising manufacturing power. Frontier markets like eastern Africa and Indonesia may well provide the next big boom.

But right up front in this discussion, I have a request: please slap any purported expert who, in this context, tosses around the phrase "BRIC"—Brazil, Russia, India, and China—as an investible class. The acronym should stand for "bloody ridiculous investment concept." Those four countries couldn't be more different in terms of education, history, natural resources, political organization, economic policies, work culture, respect for rule of law, demographics, or market outlook. Russia and Brazil thrive off high energy costs; India and China suffer by them. They don't offer essentially the same investment opportunities just because their initials form a clever moniker.

---

* For another example, see **latency arbitrage** in the glossary.

And if treating that small group as homogenous is silly, treating the other 150 or so developing and frontier markets as a unit is downright absurd. There is no automatic path to eventual emergence as a thriving market economy, as once-hot economies like Iraq, the Philippines, Pakistan, and Burma (now Myanmar, and the name change is instructive in itself) amply demonstrate. The various countries of the world will all follow their own, highly unpredictable paths. ETFs that lump them together—in any subset—are, to my mind, just misguided.

So the goal is to find precise ways to participate while minimizing exposure to minor issues like corruption, lack of investor protections, and regime change. For many investors, the smartest way in is through a few top-tier larger corporations that do business abroad and have the resources, savvy, and leverage to navigate tricky local issues and pick their own investing spots. The obvious choices here are the big U.S. companies offering products America is famous for: technology, pharmaceuticals, personal care and consumer goods, along with a couple of heavy equipment manufacturers.

But who likes obvious? Better choices may be the "global blue chips" that have grown up in China, Mexico, India, and Latin America over the past decades. It's not just that these companies know their own markets better than any U.S. company could. More important, they're often better equipped to crack other developing markets, with superior understanding of how to reach low-income consumers, how to adopt to local customs and mores, and what product changes to make to maximize appeal. As an example, the world's third-largest "white goods" manufacture is Chinese, having reached that status not because of sales in China, but rather because of the clever way it entered market after market around the rest of the world.

There are downsides to these foreign-born companies: some are controlled by small families and some are heavily influenced by governmental organs; a few have less than perfect appreciation of fiduciary duties to minority shareholders; many may not fully grasp that crazy old "dividend" concept to which we are attached.

The best suggestion here, then, is once again to pony up for professional management with one of the excellent mutual funds that focus on developing-country large caps, especially in a few select countries that seem to have the ingredients for success mostly in place: think Turkey, the Czech Republic, Poland, South Korea, and Peru. No doubt, some other earlier stage economies will produce bigger winners (probably from Africa)—but those kinds of bets don't really fit into a "risk reduction" diversification chapter.

Accredited investors have other options: country-specific hedge funds and funds of funds. These days, serious local expertise is a necessary element of any attempt at alpha. Back in the '90s, when the investment field was new, bold macroeconomists may have been able to trade them from afar with limited on-the-ground knowledge. Those days are over. Vetted local managers, with proper infrastructures and skin in the game, are the increasingly popular path toward capturing the growth, and limiting the downside, of younger economies.

Black Swans and Fat Tails

"Black swan" funds, pioneered by Nicholas Taleb (not Natalie Portman), are meant to profit hugely from very unexpected and catastrophic risks that wreak financial havoc on everyone else. The name reflects the shock of the new: in 1697, the world was stunned to learn that swans could actually be black, a fact completely unsuspected until they were discovered in Australia. The philosophy of Taleb & Co. is to be prepared to profit from similarly unexpected developments in the financial world.

The style is also called a "tail" or "fat tail" fund, referring to the long ends of the normal bell curve distribution patterns.

NORMAL DISTRIBUTION

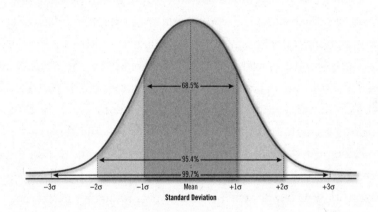

Events out at each end of this normal distribution curve are several "standard deviations" of likelihood away from those in the big part of the bell, where nearly all typical financial analysts concentrate their attention. (You can see that 99.7% of all events are within three standard deviations of the mean.) Such events don't happen often, but they certainly do happen. Pitchers do hit home runs. So Taleb's big insight was that options covering super-extreme market events were being ignored and therefore underpriced, and his strategy (handsomely rewarded) was to buy ultracheap options and wait for the hundred-year flood (now arriving monthly). In the crash, that paid off quite handsomely indeed.

Thus black swan funds usually invest in various, far-out-of-the-money derivatives and then wait for the disaster that puts them in-the-money. These may be as simple as puts on the S&P, or as complex as "protection" against sovereign debt default through credit default swaps. Whatever the exact strategy, the basic idea is homeowner's insurance on someone else's house: pay a small premium, and hope a tree falls on it.

The problem is therefore obvious: investors can go years slowly bleeding money while the world doesn't implode. Regardless of the form, options suffer "decay" . . . their value dissipates over time unless the covered event occurs, or at least threatens to. So black swan fund investors can expect to lose a few percentage points per year, in addition to the typical 1.5% or 2% management fees, in the disappointing scenario that the world manages to muddle along.

A dedicated short fund is similar but different. These guys don't necessarily need the world to blow up to do well (although mostly they're happy when it does); they're stock pickers, so in principle they can do well in most environments . . . some stocks go down even in raging bull markets. But shorting is a very, very hard thing to do well, possibly the most difficult discipline in the land of investments. Even when you're completely right about a stock being overvalued, it can stay that way, or keep moving higher, indefinitely. As the expression goes, the market can stay irrational longer than you can stay solvent.

It's a particularly tough game when you're trying to profit from technology shifts. An old but illustrative example involved Deluxe Corporation, the dominant provider of physical bank checks. In the mid–1990s it became abundantly clear that e-checks would topple the company's huge near-monopoly, and numerous short sellers, led by Jim Cramer, piled in. A complete no-brainer, right? But quarter after quarter, the company provided new news that would get the Wall Street analysts, who had no interest in reading the writing on the wall even if they could see it, another excuse to reiterate their "buy" recommendations. After a year and a half of taking bath after bath, Cramer threw in the towel . . . one quarter too soon. Management finally fessed up to the coming damage, and the stock plunged by half.

The "Bernanke put" makes shorting even tougher these days; his aggressively loose monetary policy supports the market, and fighting the Fed is a classic stock market no-no. But exactly because the strategy's been out of favor for a while might be an excellent reason to embrace it. After all, in 2008, many dedicated short funds were up 30% or 40%, a dream diversifier.

Some very famous managers make their livings this way. David Einhorn can make a stock crash by simply mentioning it in public. His Greenlight Capital was on the correct side of Lehman and Allied Capital, so when he mouthed "Chipotle" at an investor conference, the company instantly lost $600 million of market cap (another arrow into Mr. Efficient Market, who's looking a bit like St. Sebastian). The phenomenon has generated a new verb: "Einhorning" a stock.

A more conventional practitioner is Jim Chanos. He's a good bookend for this chapter, which started with long/short strategies, because you might describe his as short/long. He shorted Hewlett-Packard and Dell because he thought both companies had missed the fundamental shift away from personal computers and tried to play catch-up with risky acquisitions. But at the same time, he went long on Microsoft, because he thought it was fairly valued and was doing a good job in shifting into a cloud-based solutions company. In a way very similar to the earlier story about the disk drive companies, he wound up profiting on both sides of the trade.

Dedicated short funds run by managers of this caliber might be the best risk reducer out there. But this is yet another area where the quality of the manager is everything; most "bear market" mutual funds have been hammered in the years since the crash, even as the stars of the field have prospered.

So for typical investors, here's a simple approach. Let's call cash the poor man's black swan strategy. It won't skyrocket in a crisis, but (1) to the extent you're holding it, you're not long assets that crater; and (2) cash allows you to buy in at bottoms, so you can pick up the pieces when everyone else has to liquidate at whatever they can get. That this is a wise approach is validated by no less a figure than the legendary hedge fund manager Seth Klarman, whose firm Baupost Group has one of the very best long-term records in history. He often keeps large chunks of capital in cash, 30% or even 50%. That meant that in 2008 Baupost was one of the few firms with enough available capital to vacuum up the assets being tossed overboard at fire sale prices. Says he: "The ability to offer one-stop shopping for an urgent seller is very advantageous."

In Review

An attractive set of long/short mutual funds can deliver the prototypical hedged investing strategy to anyone. Some do make the investments internally, while some allocate to outside experts that are running these sorts of strategies.

On the private placement side, funds of funds are pricey but can be worth it, especially to get at otherwise inaccessible smaller managers running niche strategies or local managers in emerging economies. What matters is simply the returns after all fees.

Farmland is a super source of uncorrelated income and inflation protection. Its price has run up lately, but it remains an intriguing long-term investment for both its strong diversification characteristics and its inflation protection.

Managed futures are the newest major branch of alternatives, but have shown some of the best performance in adverse markets.

"Global blue chips" are probably the best way to get exposure to the high-growth frontier markets. They can navigate the inevitable instability that comes from rapid development in previously poor societies.

Black swan funds do well when the world goes haywire but are expensive insurance when it doesn't. Dedicated short funds are probably a better idea for downside protection. And then there's the easy way: just hold plenty of cash.

Final Thought

The single biggest thing average investors can do to improve their portfolios is to add protection against adverse stock market moves. The numerous new smart beta products, especially mutual funds of funds that aggregate various long/short managers, deserve a close look by almost everyone.

CHAPTER 7

Long-Term Growth Enhancement (Job 3)

Global Macro	Distressed	Activist	Venture Funds
Angel	O&G Drilling	PE Secondaries	Growth PE

It seems to be a law of nature, inflexible and inexorable, that those who will not risk cannot win.

—JOHN PAUL JONES

Time to play offense. These are the strategies through which John Paulson generated a 500% return for his investors in a year and that returned George Soros 6,000% over ten. It's where private company investors routinely talk about getting multiples of their money back instead of basis points on it. Much of that potential upside comes from the strategies themselves, but this is also where we'll find some superstar managers who really produce alpha.

There is just a touch of bad news that we should get out of the way up front. Although there are liquid alternatives that address some of these strategies, the majority come in private placement form, and so require committing dollars for at least some period of time (from one year to several). That's because these styles just take a while to reach fruition, and because the best managers require locked-up money to go to work. But of course that's a key reason the opportunities exist. Not everyone can participate, so those who can have an advantage. And if you're tempted to shy away from these ideas merely because of the lack of liquidity, please first take a peek ahead to chapter 9, and consider the liquidity ratio and model portfolio discussions there.

As you can guess, on a stand-alone basis, some of these approaches also involve a higher degree of risk than, say, a long/short strategy. But approached intelligently, and inside a balanced portfolio appropriate to your resources, they can very meaningfully increase long-term returns.

We'll start the chapter with three styles that are "semiliquid" and then move on to the really long-term strategies. First up, the strategies that made hedge funds famous, the one where they go hunting with elephant guns.

Global Macro Funds

On September 16, 1992, George Soros and Julian Robertson broke the Bank of England. It was the signature event of the modern hedge fund era.

The UK had joined Europe's "Exchange Rate Mechanism" two years earlier, promising to keep the value of the pound within limits set in relation to the German deutsche mark. To do that, it was forced to adopt very strict anti-inflationary measures—which meant high interest rates that the big hedge funds of the day, led by Soros, didn't believe could be maintained in the face of a slow economy. They bet heavily that the UK would ultimately have to breach the ERM and let its currency fall versus the mark, and accumulated massive positions against the currency with forwards, futures, and puts.

That created a wave of selling that kept pushing the currency to the limits set forth in the ERM agreement. Finally, the bank launched a vicious counterattack, buying a massive £15 billion sterling in the open market. Like a gallant charge by the Confederacy, it was brave but not enough . . . the selling continued, and the value kept falling. Now in a panic, the bank resorted to a last stand on September 16, jacking interest rates up 5% in one go to strengthen the currency . . . only to watch it set new lows. That night, the white flag went up, and the UK announced it would leave the ERM. The pound lost 13% of its value over the next ten days, netting Soros over $1 billion . . . at the time, a lot of money. So was born the image of hedge fund manager as wild gunslinger.

These days, adding a global macro strategy to your portfolio is important for a very specific reason: governmental policies have become central drivers of world finance and business. In the United States and Europe, postcrisis central bank and executive branch policies are at least as influential in the markets as the fundamental economic forces that underpin efficient market theory. And in China—well, you know, you have that good old-fashioned Communist central planning thing happening. Global macro strategists specialize in foreseeing, understanding, and exploiting the resulting trading opportunities.

Thus, the most recent fodder for the global macro crowd includes the never-ending Eurozone crisis, a slowdown (or not) in China, the Fed's zero interest rate policies, tax changes, too-big-to-fail banks, and the rest of the government-business tango. But they also trade trends like global weather disruptions and the resulting pressure on food prices, military flare-ups that threaten oil supply risks, and the impact of upcoming elections. They trade in every market through every kind of instrument, from futures and forwards to options to credit default swaps.

Many of these strategies in some way involve currencies; one of the most famous is the so-called **carry trade**. The idea is to borrow in a country where the interest rates are low and invest the proceeds in a country where interest rates are high. So an investor would borrow, say, Japanese yen at essentially zero interest rate and invest the proceeds in, say, Australian dollar bonds at maybe 4%. A $10 million trade would net you $400,000 while you do nothing at all.

So where's the risk? Well, if the exchange rates don't change, you're fine. And if the yen depreciates against the Australian dollar, you're really in super shape. But if the yen appreciates against the Aussie, you can get in the hole very, very quickly, because it's going to take a lot more Aussie dollars to buy back the yen necessary to repay the loan. And the kicker is that economic theory tells you that's exactly what *should* happen: it says the reason that one currency has a high interest rate is that it is compensating investors for an expected decrease in its value.

But that's obviously not what the folks putting on the trade expect . . . and, more to the point, they think they're smart enough to see a yen appreciation coming, and unwind the trade quickly when that's on the horizon. But of course everyone in the trade thinks that, and they can't all be first out. That's what makes it interesting, and is one reason why the currency markets are so volatile.

Given the inherently noncorrelated returns these strategies provide, and their suitability for a world in which governmental policies play a bigger role than normal, this field is a top choice for alternative investors. And because many of the very best hedge fund managers are global macro guys, it is also a promising place to look for alpha and outperformance.

For those who cannot afford any illiquidity at all, there are some good mutual funds that do follow global macro–type strategies. These can serve as excellent diversifiers; just don't expect to clear the bases with them.

Activist Funds

Activist funds are also fertile ground in the alpha hunt, and have been drawing more than their fair share of pension plan investors over the past couple of years. The simple reason is that they've been turning in better annualized returns than the overall markets . . . almost 10% per year. That number tracks several academic studies that have shown that activist targets have meaningfully outperformed the overall markets

In the lingo of activists, each investment is a "campaign." Once a meaningful stake in a company has been accumulated, the fund managers contact management and file a form 13D with the SEC, which puts the world on notice that the game is afoot. (Some traders are always on the prowl for new 13Ds and start buying stock in the target as soon as they see one filed.) From there, company management can effectively concede that they are willing to accept the "help" and work with the activists in what then becomes a "constructive activist" deal, or they can resist, and start generating headlines as the fight escalates.

In a book about alternatives, it is perhaps a bit odd to highlight a traded stock strategy that boils down to an intense long-only play (very few activist managers actually short stock). But these funds' "risk management" comes from the hard work their managers inject into the company after they've taken a position in it. Moreover, these funds are good examples of **horizon arbitrage** . . . with everyone so focused on short-term results, funds that specialize in longer-term values probably have an edge.

In thinking about activist funds, one big issue to consider is how well the category of targets might hold up in a major market reversal. Many activists were hammered in the crash for a pretty obvious reason: they were, by definition, investing in poorly managed companies, which naturally suffered the most from the resulting "flight to quality." Big caps tend to fare better than small caps in those periods, and companies with lots of cash on the balance sheet do best. Investing with managers who vet their targets with that in mind may be the least risky way to approach the field.

Once again, the top managers significantly outperform the rest of the field, and here the reasons are obvious. Prosecuting a campaign to extract maximum value is truly a combination of hard work, skill, legal expertise, and timing. Returns from the top activist funds are often impressive.

There are some decent liquid choices available here, specifically mutual funds that specialize in buying stocks after a 13D has been filed, and the results so far support the theory that this is a promising investment strategy. Even in this format, though, investors should expect to stay in a good while to see the benefits. The big joke around the alternatives watercooler is that activist hedge funds are "PE in drag."

"Distressed" Funds

Bernie Madoff lost a lot of money for hedge fund investors; did you know he made a lot for them, too? He did, really; just not his own. As discussed when we introduced distressed investing back in chapter 3, it turns out that bankruptcy court is another place where a savvy eye, deep knowledge of the rules, patience, and hard work can produce whopping returns.

In Mr. Madoff's case, all sorts of people had claims against him after the fall. What were they worth? Not much, unless the bankruptcy trustee could force the investors who pulled cash out before the scandal broke to give it back. Would he be successful? How successful? When?

Most claim holders just didn't have the expertise to evaluate these questions, or the stomach to sit around while they got decided. But many hedge fund managers specialize in exactly this process. Some did a deep dive and concluded that decent recoveries were actually fairly likely. They bought up claims from burned investors at big discounts to their face amounts, and that paid off hugely when the trustee was indeed successful in recouping money from the innocent, but wrongly enriched, investors who redeemed out of the Madoff fund early.

But perhaps the greatest bankruptcy-based trade ever was General Growth Properties, the giant mall operator, after what the *New York Times* called "one of the biggest commercial real estate collapses in history." GGP's stock had fallen 97% by the time it filed for Chapter 11 in April 2009, a consequence of high vacancy rates and the impending due dates of too many short-term mortgages.

But its stellar properties, like Water Tower Place in Chicago,

Ala Moana Center in Honolulu, and Faneuil Hall in Boston, were just too juicy for Bill Ackman to ignore. His Pershing Square Capital teamed up with others to recapitalize the company, and I guess you could say that it's turned out pretty well: so far, the return is something like eighty *times* the initial investment.

That bankruptcy court is where some of the biggest fortunes await is definitely ironic. But if you don't mind profiting from the misfortunes of others, consider a distressed fund. By definition, these are purchasing debt or equity securities that have already lost huge chunks of value, so the downside risk is often contained, and in the hands of experienced managers who know the bankruptcy process, the upsides can be substantial. This is another area in which accredited investors have an advantage; it's difficult for liquid alternatives managers to hold these kinds of securities, or to work them to full value. But some "event driven" mutual funds do exist, and a few sport nice track records.

Illiquid Investments

The next few entries share some common characteristics that are worth discussing up front. You already know that private equity, venture, and angel investing can provide some extraordinary longer term returns, which is great, but investing in them usually requires ongoing funding over time, which is not. You do not have to invest great fortunes to participate in some of these deals, but remember that they are marriages, not dates. For most of them, in fact, you have to endure the "pain of the J curve." It's a sort of modern financial torture technique.

Here's a picture that's not so pretty:

THE J CURVE

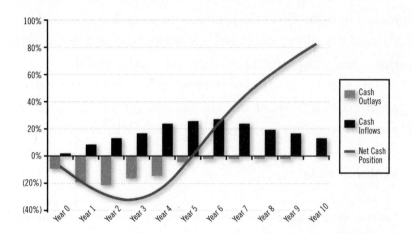

The lighter bars are cash out of pocket, the darker ones cash returns. The line is the investor's net cash position; as you can see, it resembles the letter *J*.

This is a function of how PE and venture funds work: the fund manager gets commitments from investors, say for $1 million each. But they don't put up the whole million right away because the fund can't spend it right away . . . the managers have to go find and lock up deals first.

So the actual cash investments are staged to match up with how quickly the fund can spend the committed dollars. On a million-dollar commitment, the investor may only put in, say, $300k. After the fund invests that money, it will issue "calls" for more capital (the investors either make good on their commitments or are penalized). And the investors also have to keep putting up the money to pay the management fees, the 2%.

And since it takes a while to fix up an acquired company (or in the case of a VC, to go from start-up to exit), the fund can't sell its investments for a while. Thus, early in the fund cycle, the investors keep writing checks for a good while before anything comes back. That's the dip in the J. Of course, you're hoping that down the road those investments will pay off, and the total dollars back will exceed those invested . . . that's the backbone of the J.

J curve or no, this class of investments is a top source of outsize returns. Good funds of this class should generate 2x to 4x the original investment over several years, with IRRs over 20%.

Venture Funds

Venture capital funds are like basketball: a true American invention. The blend of risk capital, expertise, and ferocious entrepreneurial spirit could only have been born here. (George W. Bush may have gone slightly overboard on the point when he famously claimed that the French have no word for *entrepreneur*, but you know what he meant.) Applied to the fertile ground of technology innovation, it has produced countless world-changing companies. In a perfect world, that should generate gargantuan profits; even in our very imperfect one, it does.

Those opportunities continue to abound; certainly, the pace of revolutionary changes isn't slowing down any. Robotics and 3D printing are poised for their glory days (did you know that Bond's Aston Martin in *Skyfall*, blown up at the end, was a replica made with a 3D printer? That's why they could afford to shoot the scene repeatedly). Mobile devices, the cloud, and voice recognition will profoundly alter the ways in which we use computers. Two massive industries, education and health care, are already reinventing themselves to exploit technology to reduce costs; others will follow. Global Internet penetration will continue to skyrocket, and transactional dollar volumes will follow as the rest of the world cultures become more comfortable with providing sensitive information online and as nonbank payment systems become ever more available.

Meantime, though, the number of dollars raised by venture capital firms has been falling for several years (to about $18 billion in 2011 from over $30 billion in 2007). That's a good thing if you can get your money to work in the right deals, since it clearly means more opportunities at better prices. Equally important, an excellent exit path, much more reliable than the traditional IPO, has emerged of late: an enormous herd of strategic buyers. As large companies build huge cash war chests, but slash R&D spending, they're essentially forced to go out shopping for important innovations. In the '80s, about nine out of ten exits were IPOs, and just 10% were through merger transaction; today, that ratio is almost exactly reversed.

The downside of investing in venture funds is pretty simple: many don't do so well. Study after study indicates that the top 10% of funds generate a hugely disproportionate share of the entire industry's returns, and that many funds in the bottom half of performance statistics have failed to return all of their investors' dollars. There's a pretty clear reason: deal flow. Nothing succeeds like success, and entrepreneurs very much want to work with the VC firms that have big wins on their belts. The same is true even with the numerous new seed-stage funds, which are making smaller bets faster than their more established cousins . . . a few top-tier funds have emerged very quickly.

It's pretty easy to find those top performers, but they're not taking new capital from strangers, so don't bother to call. Obviously nothing says previously poorly performing funds, or new ones, won't do just fine, but figuring out which ones are good bets probably requires a pretty high level of expertise in the space. Therefore, a top-quality fund of funds can be a smart move here.

Several of these can still get "capacity" from the best VC funds, and have excellent track records even after taking account of the additional level of fees.

Angel Investing

Venture capital funds dominated the start-up landscape for many decades, but direct individual angel investing is now the most dynamic segment of the alternative universe. It's experiencing an ongoing revolution that has taken it from a casual game of the superwealthy to a deeply professional activity that invests over $20 billion every year in U.S. start-ups, and much more around the world.

The biggest reason is the jaw-dropping reduction in the amount of capital necessary to get a venture off the ground. Twenty years ago, it might have taken $20 million to start a company; ten years ago, $2 million; now it often takes as few as tens of thousands. The Internet, open-source software, outsourcing, app stores, search advertising, and social media have reduced every cost dramatically, from development to telecommunications to marketing and distribution. One example: over the last two decades, the price of storing one gigabyte of data is down from $70,000 to about twenty-five cents.

That means that seed funding of start-ups is now within the financial reach of many investors, and easy for small groups of them. One study pegs the average per company per "angel" investment at around $25,000, with groups of angels combining to invest maybe $250,000 in a given company.

Equally important has been the enormous improvement in the infrastructure of angel investing, starting with the proliferation and professionalization of angel groups. Most of these arose as clubs of slightly bored rich people, but they've now morphed into ad hoc VC firms, with standardized due diligence practices, deal flow management, and negotiation processes. An enabling and parallel development has been the creation of platforms and tools for finding deals, evaluating companies, and managing investments, within and across angel groups. Gust.com, the brainchild of industry pioneer David S. Rose, demonstrates just how powerful the trend is. Each month, several thousand early-stage companies create Web-based investor presentations from the site's templates; and, globally, many tens of thousands of angels, angel groups, and seed-stage venture funds sort through them, looking for investments.* Angellist.com is a somewhat similar platform, particularly popular among the Silicon Valley crowd.

Angel investing is a fun world, full of smart people and cool companies. Funnily enough, that's a bit of a problem, for it's easy to fall into doing it as a hobby and making a couple of random investments per year just to stay in the club. That's a wonderful way to pass the time, but not a great way to make money. Remember how we've talked about "alpha" being mostly a function of hard work? It is. And in the seed funding world, you're doing an awful lot of it.

For those who are serious about it, there are two basic approaches. The more traditional is to invest only in fields you know well, a handful of companies at a time, with the expectation of helping out personally (that's me). You might call this the Keynesian school of angel investing, given his view that "[a]s time goes on, I get more and more convinced that the right method of investment is to put fairly large sums into enterprises which one thinks one knows something about and in the management of which one thoroughly believes."

---

* Perhaps some bias here; sorry, I'm on the board.

But a professional class of angel investors has now emerged who take more of a true portfolio approach, just as VCs do. They spread their investments across many companies every year, expecting to lose money on a large number, break even on a few, and hit one or two gushers. The data isn't deep, but several industry studies show that these serious angels can do quite well, with average returns of over 2x their investments over periods of three to four years. In other words, somewhere in the same ballpark as the better VC firms.

Either way, a huge piece of the puzzle is keeping plenty of powder dry for follow on rounds and new opportunities. The biggest mistake new investors make is to max out on their per-company investment in its first round, or their per-year budget on one deal. Nearly always, the companies in which you have invested will be back for more capital (and if you don't play in those next rounds, you'll be badly diluted). Indeed, angel investing is a lot like Texas Hold-em, with many rounds of decisions before the jackpot gets claimed. So plan accordingly.

Affiliation with a regional or industry-focused angel group is the best way to get involved. As a way to learn the ropes, there's just nothing like hearing experienced investors evaluate candidate companies. There are many hundreds of groups around the world, with the most professional belonging to organizations such as the Angel Capital Association in the United States, the National Angel Capital Organization in Canada, or EBAN in Europe. The entertaining people you'll meet are a bonus.

Now, what about the hot topic of the day, "crowdfunding"? This is the idea that start-ups attract capital from neither VCs nor angels, but instead through numerous very small investors brought together through Internet portals. A core principle is that the "wisdom of crowds" will operate to correctly select good new companies from bad ones, and that, as a result, the process of capital formation will be hugely expedited. All very noble.

This story was so appealing that it got Republicans and Democrats to rush a sweeping bill through Congress in 2012, the so-called JOBS Act, that eliminated several securities laws provisions that stood in the way. That was impressive, since at the time the two parties could not agree on whether it was a good idea to have air traffic controllers or pay veterans' benefits. Even the most cynical politicians couldn't ignore the siren call of spontaneous, Web-based business formation, new jobs, and less government regulation and involvement.

And over time, there's every reason to think the venture/angel funding ecosystem will evolve to accommodate crowdfunding. But I'd sit it out for now. It's not so much the much-discussed potential for outright fraud . . . the Web's reputation systems do generally seem to work, as eBay and Amazon show. Instead, the question is how to get the crowdfunding capital-raising rounds done in a way that will make sense for the original funders and still allow the start-up to access the more traditional capital sources that it will normally require later.

If, for example, the initial crowdfunded valuation for a company is too high (very possible, especially if the trend becomes popular), subsequent VC and angel investors may stay away: who's going to want a bunch of angry, crammed-down small investors as co-shareholders? Frankly, just having a large number of small shareholders in the company is itself a turnoff for professional investors. Decisions that are already difficult and get made in the process of growing a young company, like management changes, might well become far more of a political process than professional investors will want to face.

All that said, what should you look for in a start-up as an angel investor? Here are my five threshold issues:

1. Management Team. Is this really more important than the core idea or business plan? Absolutely. Things are just moving so fast that many business plans are outdated within months. Moreover, you simply don't know what the market is going to like or not like about the basic idea until it's out there—product modifications will be required, pricing will have to be adjusted, customer acquisition plans will change. The single most important ingredient of success is having a management team in place that has impeccable integrity, can iterate the product quickly, pivot the business model as necessary, and keep costs down in the process. One of the most common phrases you'll hear from experienced angel investors is that you're betting on the jockey, not the horse.

2. Funding Risk. This is the single biggest risk any start-up faces: will it be able to get to self-sustaining mode before it runs out of cash? Of course, this requires focus on the company's revenue model (yes, it should have one!), the costs involved in getting there, and the cash on hand.

There are two massively important points here. The first is that the start-up should be far more than an inspiration. As the uncle of the venture world, Howard Morgan, likes to joke, there are two kinds of seed investments: those that are too early, and those that are way too early. You can help yourself avoid the second camp by requiring entrepreneurs to demonstrate some sort of working prototype and a hint of market acceptance (in the parlance, "traction") before injecting capital. Don't invest in mere ideas.

Just as important is the existence of a bona fide revenue model. Especially for new angels, this point cannot be overstated. Professional investors can take the risks on social media start-ups without a revenue model, but that is a trick that you should not try at home. Maybe this is a bit of a West Coast (build it and we'll figure out monetization later) versus East Coast (show me the money!) thing, but I'm from New York. Here, we like to tell the story about the new bar that opened in Silicon Valley: it's absolutely jam-packed every single night because all the drinks are free, and the backers are ecstatic.

Aside from the obvious, a profoundly important reason to only invest in start-ups with real revenue models is that the outside funding environment can change in a heartbeat. When the last crash arrived, a lot of promising young companies hit the wall because there was simply no new cash available for the next round. If the company's plan is to keep developing products and then go raise more capital, without revenue in sight, be careful.

3. Scalability: Is the concept a company, a product, or a feature? Many wonderful ideas are simply not robust enough to build an entire company around; at best, they can evolve into a product with a limited audience, or maybe they're even just a nice enhancement to an existing offering. The companion question is: how large is the target market? Precision is not necessary—or even possible—but you do want to know the market is a very big one, ideally large enough to absorb multiple entrants. That's because it's a sure bet someone else is working on the same idea—if not, it's probably a bad one. "We have absolutely no competi-

tion!" induces a reaction in investors that is exactly opposite to the one that entrepreneurs think it does.

4. **Defensibility.** Of course you want to fund a start-up whose idea can't be immediately knocked off by just anyone. But at the same time, it's not generally reasonable to expect you'll be protected by patents or other formal IP. From a purely practical point of view, that's too expensive, slow, and actually pretty ineffective unless you have some awesome, free lawyers hanging around. The main protection is usually the speed with which it is implemented and then iterated (another reason number 1 is reason 1).

5. Exit Strategy. And not via an IPO. What's most realistic these days is an exit via sale to an existing major company for which you solve a meaningful problem. Most large enterprises now look at outside start-ups as a substitute for a portion of their R & D budget, and the large tech companies, for example, are all sitting on tens of billions of dollars. Shooting for that sort of exit over a three- to five-year period is often a decent plan.

There's much more on angel investing, including what sorts of documentation to use for the actual investment, in chapter 10.

AN INSTRUCTIVE COMPARISON: KLEINER PERKINS VERSUS GSV

There's a lot to learn by comparing these two groups. They do both invest in pre-public companies. But one is an iconic brand that has generated unimaginable fortunes for its investors; the other is a train wreck.

Kleiner Perkins essentially invented the modern VC firm. Instead of looking only at companies with a fully baked plans and complete management teams, it would jump in early and became a full participant in value creation. Aside from funding, they'd toss in executives, relationships, technology, and every manner of support. As cofounder Tom Perkins loves to point out, money is the most fungible of all commodities; if that's all you're bringing to the table, there are an infinite number of competitors who can do the same thing. Smart entrepreneurs want a lot more than cash from their VC partners.

GSV, on the other hand, is a closed-end fund that bought shares of companies like Facebook, Zynga, and Groupon after they were fully flowered, but before they went public. Actually, to call GSV a "venture capital" firm, as the press often does, is a stretch. In fact, most of the time GSV was actually writing the checks by which the real venture capitalists were exiting the investment (*never* a good sign!). The antithesis of KP, it added absolutely zero value to the target companies (and indeed could not possibly even value the investment it was making, since the companies weren't disclosing their financials in the process). GSV was quite literally an objective exercise in the greater fool theory. The hundred lashes it has since received from the market were well and truly deserved.

You'll remember our definition of alpha: value created by hard work. The KP-GSV tale is another example.

Private Equity

Like the venture and angel categories, private equity focuses on nonpublic securities and projects. The mechanics of the traditional leveraged buyout fund were described in chapter 3, and you can see how, in the right economic environment, they can do exceedingly well.

But: they do use a lot of debt, which adds major risks to a transaction. If the economy slows so that turnaround timelines can't be met, and the debt on the enterprise can't be easily refinanced, you'll have a sequel to the horror movie of 2008. At the moment, another issue also looms large, which is the tremendous amount of "dry powder" that PE firms have and are all looking to spend in the next year or two. There are too many very well financed buyers chasing too few deals: that's a bad omen, especially since the waters, at least in the United States, have already been pretty thoroughly fished.

Therefore, at a minimum, investors in traditional-style PE funds should be very selective. One thing to look for is a management team with proven expertise at increasing top-line revenues in their target companies. In a slow-growth environment where bargains are nearly impossible to find, real profits will most frequently be driven by the PE firm's ability to increase the post-investment top line of its targets. Potential investors may also want to look for firms with mid- and smaller-market focus (where auctions are less common) or a niche strategy, like focus on a demographic group, geography, or industry.

But some kinds of PE funds look much more interesting than the classic LBO style these days. One is growth PE; the other is PE secondaries.

Growth PE Funds

"Growth capital" PE firms can make a lot of sense. As you might guess, these are kissing cousins of later-stage venture outfits, except that they tend to invest in a much broader array of businesses: retail, financial, food, light manufacturing. Many times, these deals are less risky than the classic LBO transactions for the simple reason that they use less debt and more equity (sometimes, 100% equity, at least until the target reaches a certain level of profitability). Some of the more successful growth PE funds specialize in specific markets; a niche approach can provide important industry relationship and deal flow advantages.

As one example, let's take a real-world PE firm that focuses on young orthopedic device companies. These things are typically invented by surgeons around the country in the course of their normal practices; the doctors discover that they require a new tool for conducting a kind of surgery, or a new kind of implant for a specific condition. That's where the real "R & D" in the space occurs; there is no Silicon Valley for medical devices.

Very often, the doctor will start a small company, get the device manufactured by a specialty house, and get any necessary approvals. This PE firm usually hears about all this early on and, assuming things look good, tries to buy the company after it's had a bit of success but before it hits everybody's radar screen. It then injects capital, management expertise, and distribution help. With luck, the new company grows to a decent size and then is sold off to one of the medical device giants, which typically look to smaller companies like this for innovative new products—for them, it's outsourced R & D.

Arguably, that's "private equity" at its best, using capital and brains to accelerate delivery of better medical devices to the market. If they make a ton of money along the way, more power to them.

Secondary PE Funds

As you know, during the golden era of private equity early in this century, many PE firms and investors simply made a killing. That created the inevitable cycle: hundreds of competitors were formed, MBAs flocked in, and banks fell over themselves for the rich fees and fat yields generated by the necessary loans.

The result was quite predictable. Too much money chasing too few quality deals meant targets got overpaid for, and overleveraged. When the music stopped in 2008, big percentages of these transactions went off the tracks and still haven't recovered. Indeed, many investors who expected to be out long ago are still trapped inside funds that are themselves sitting on underwater positions. Some funds are so far from ever returning investor capital that they're called "zombies."

Many investors in such funds are seeking to sell their partnership positions at a big discount. Some really need the cash, but many are simply trying to rebalance their portfolios into more liquid assets as a result of the aforementioned denominator effect.

Several funds have sprung up to take advantage, and they present strong benefits to their own investors. First, they're buying seasoned interests, so they're getting to see an existing deal portfolio, rather than investing in a blind pool up front. Second, they are investing after time has already passed on the underlying investments, so that dip in the J, if still there, is shorter and shallower. Third, when they buy secondaries from many different funds, they've effectively created a fund of PE funds, typically increasing geographic and industry diversification. And fourth, of course, is that big discount they negotiate with the seller.

As a result, while the crash was certainly a disaster for traditional PE investors, it might have opened an interesting door for those who can suffer the necessary illiquidity. To help you summon up the courage, note that mighty Yale actually increased its allocation to PE after the crash, on the theory (historically correct) that the best "vintage years" of PE deals follow the worst ones. Its point is that success in these sorts of investments should be measured over years, not quarters. If you share that outlook, and can afford to park some money away for a while, a secondary PE fund might be a good fit.

O&G Drilling Programs

From chapter 5, you already know a bit about one way to make money from energy exploration. The owner of a royalty interest buys it for a fixed amount and is entitled to a specified revenue stream from the property.

A different approach, one with a lot more upside, is a "working interest." Owners of working interests are responsible for the costs of exploration, drilling, and production of a project. As a result, they own a much greater piece of the economic upside, usually with major tax breaks that sweeten the effective yield.

Numerous private partnerships offer investors pieces of working interests of oil and gas wells, although the details can be very, very different. Sometimes investors become general partners (more risks, more tax benefits), sometimes they take a more traditional limited partner (and limited liability) role. Return projections, of course, also vary wildly. But it is not unreasonable to look to double or possibly triple your money over the course of three to five years (that is, with IRRs in the twenties), without taking crazy risks . . . so long as oil and gas prices don't take a big tumble from here.

By not taking crazy risks, I mean investing in very high-probability projects with proven sponsors. It is not difficult to locate programs run by an experienced team, operating in fields and rock types where they have proven track records. The science has improved radically over the years, and with many projects the odds of dry holes are remote, although the total production and ultimate economics are uncertain.

As usual, the details of the investment partnership are absolutely crucial. Ideally, the investor should receive all his investment back before the sponsor's carried interest kicks in; one common pattern is for the investor to receive 125% of his capital back before a sponsor's 25% or 30% performance fee is collected. There are far too many subtleties to address here (one example: the sponsor should not own an overriding royalty interest in the project), so you should work with very well respected sponsors and do your homework. But all in all, if you're an accredited investor looking for significant upside through a reasonable gamble, this is a sector to investigate.

Nonaccredited investors can look to a few mutual funds that specialize in companies holding working interests rather than royalties, and also invest in more exotic energy investments, like oil sands. Some of these have done extremely well. There are also a couple of publicly traded finance companies out there—one that's managed by KKR, for example—that hold substantial interests in natural resources via working interests. These liquid instruments are interesting ways to play the commodity and energy game, but they don't pass through the tax benefits and certainly do not have the same upside potential as investing through private partnership structures.

In Review

....

Global macro managers, the all-purpose opportunists of the hedge fund world, can provide real pop to portfolios and also deliver powerful noncorrelation benefits.

Activist and distressed investment funds are two more places to look for alpha. In both, managers work directly to improve the value of securities they hold. Privately placed partnerships dominate the investment opportunities, but there are "event driven" mutual funds out there that focus on these strategies.

The single best place to look for grand slam returns may be in early-stage companies. It's difficult to pick winners from the legions of start-ups, but the best venture capital groups do it regularly. While the top funds are mostly closed to new investors, they can often be accessed through funds of funds with "capacity," which should, therefore, be worth the extra fee layer.

If you've got the time and energy to do it yourself, a disciplined program of angel investing can be intellectually and socially rewarding, and the better angels earn returns similar to those of established venture capital outfits.

The best opportunities in private equity may be in "secondary" funds, which recycle limited partnership interests from PE investors who need to sell. And the best feature of these is probably a shortened J curve.

Finally, there's the Texas classic: oil and gas partnerships.

Macro conditions and technology advances mean well-run private O&G partnerships can fire up a portfolio.

Final Thought

We're entering a new age of innovation now, with robotics and 3D printers set to fundamentally transform us into a post-scarcity economy. Oddly, perhaps, the last wave of tech innovation—social networking–type companies—did a lot to improve users' happiness but not so much for true, society-wide value creation. The next wave promises to be very different, and having a stake in those sorts of enterprises might just provide a winning ticket.

CHAPTER 8

Purchase Power Protection (Job 4)

Timber	Gold	Water	RE sponsor equity
Art	TIPS	Infrastructure	Collectibles

When I was young, I used to think money was the most important thing. But now that I'm old, I'm sure of it.
—OSCAR WILDE

If you've accumulated some wealth, congratulations. Now, for the hard part: keeping it.

Everyone understands that inflation, the stealthiest thief of wealth, is a risk at this point, and perhaps even a goal of some central bankers. If that doesn't sound all that scary to you, take a moment on this extended quote from John Maynard Keynes, whose name is very often (and very often incorrectly) invoked in support of ultra-easy monetary policies:

By a continuing process of inflation, governments can confiscate, secretly and unobserved, an important part of the wealth of their citizens. By this method they not only confiscate, but they confiscate arbitrarily; and, while the process impoverishes many, it actually enriches some . . . . As the inflation proceeds and the real value of the currency fluctuates wildly from month to month, all permanent relations between debtors and creditors, which form the ultimate foundation of capitalism, become so utterly disordered as to be almost meaningless; and the process of wealth-getting degenerates into a gamble and a lottery. Lenin was certainly right. There is no subtler, no surer means of overturning the existing basis of society than to debauch the currency. The process engages all the hidden forces of economic law on the side of destruction, and does it in a manner which not one man in a million is able to diagnose.*

Sobering stuff. And yet it's very difficult to see how inflation won't be the world's governments' paymaster of last resort. All politics aside (really), we are committed to years of exceedingly low interest rates from the Fed and, nearly certainly, the European Central Bank and Bank of Japan as well; and China must maintain a cheap currency to foster exports and prevent social unrest.

Meanwhile, our gross national debt—that is, money owed to outsiders, plus promises made to social programs—is somewhere around $16 trillion. That number is nearly impossible to comprehend. But, just for fun, let's take a whack at a "trillion."

A million seconds is twelve days. A billion seconds is thirty-one years. A trillion seconds ago, you might have been sharing a nice mastodon at a neighborhood cookout with Neanderthals: 29,000 B.C. Or try this. Imagine that the sum of $10 million is just one inch long. On that scale, the current gross national debt is a marathon.

---

* John Maynard Keynes, *The Economic Consequences of the Peace* (New York: Cosimo Classics, 2005), 235–36.

Solving that issue through painful tax increases and social program cuts has proved impossible to swallow, and that's unlikely to change. From the government's point of view, inflation is the spoonful of sugar that makes the medicine go down: printing money, which requires no plebiscite and no congressional approval, is the unlocked door.

The obvious conclusion is that serious inflation could be just around the corner. And a corollary is that the dollar really does have a chance of losing its status as the world's reserve currency. Paper money really is, at bottom, the ultimate confidence game, and when people stop believing, they stop believing.

RESERVE CURRENCY STATUS DOES NOT LAST FOREVER

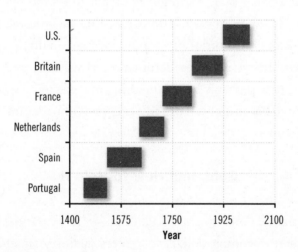

Source: J.P. Morgan

Lesson: parking your wealth exclusively in dollar-based financial assets might be akin to building a snowman in March.

Beyond all that, the basic idea of entrusting long-term wealth protection strictly to our ever more complex and fragile financial system is looking a little dicey these days. The tremors have already been felt: high-frequency trading caused the "flash crash," embarrassed the NASDAQ in the Facebook IPO, and in a happy bit of poetic justice, wiped out the equity holders of Knight Capital, a leader in the field when its computers ran amok making losing trades and couldn't be turned off (to this day nobody's explained why literally pulling the plug wasn't tried). Highly questionable practices such as "rehypothication" create crazy daisy chains of collateral among financial institutions from which the original depositor may never recover his assets, one reason why many Lehman and MF Global customers still haven't recovered their funds and perhaps never will. And let's not mention criminal and terrorist cyber attacks.

With all that said, we might not want to do too much complaining. Many aristocratic families in Europe hung on to their wealth through centuries of invading armies, multiple-currency regimes, shifting religious dominance, pestilence, and plague. Actually, they probably have something to teach us . . . which is a good thing, because this looks like one tough final exam.

Gold, and How to Hold It

Is gold a good "investment"? I don't know: is insurance? In both cases you're spending dollars to protect against something you very much hope doesn't happen.

Obviously, the one great and undeniable benefit of gold is that, over many centuries and indeed throughout human history, it has generally retained its value against the vagaries of paper currencies. Of course, nearly all paper currencies were tied directly or indirectly to precious metals, right up until Richard Nixon broke off the convertibility of dollars into gold in 1971. When he did that, and the many holders of dollars around the world could no longer call in at Fort Knox for a swap into the metal, Treasury Secretary John Connally prophetically said: "Now, it's our currency, and your problem."

Now, there is quite an active little argument about whether gold actually "is money." It certainly has some fantastic characteristics that make it a natural candidate for that role: it is extremely difficult and expensive to produce, so there are natural limits on how much is created (it takes about 250 metric tons of rock to generate enough gold for a wedding ring). It is also incredibly durable; the oft-quoted statistic is that 98% of the gold ever produced in history is still kicking around civilization in some form or another (although I don't know how anyone has figured that out). And gold is fungible, easily divisible, measurable, and, at least in small amounts, transportable. These physical properties, along with the somewhat inexplicable innate human fascination with the metal, have made it the default store of value over centuries. There's nothing like it.

Sure, it's an asset that you can treat as a standard investment if you want, and on which you can speculate if you so desire. But keep in mind that many pros have perished when blinded by its shine, just like the countless explorers who've died on their quests. The famous John Paulson, who made an incredible fortune when he was right about the subprime bubble, gave half of it right back by falling in love with Au.

So gold is insurance in this book. Whether that qualifies it as an investment, or merely a smart thing to do, is just semantics. But do remember that nobody would recommend paying lavish insurance premiums without something to insure. Same with gold.

There are many ways to buy that insurance. The most popular is with gold ETFs, which now hold close to $100 billion of the stuff. You should know that my friends who are true gold bugs don't love this approach. They make the not totally crazy argument that, if you're buying insurance against the collapse of the financial system, why buy it through that system, which would have to be the mechanism to deliver the benefit?

So they would have you own the gold in physical form, in coins or bullion. It's a little weird to have the postman deliver a small cardboard box full of gold to your door, but that's what happens . . . a whole new reason for plain, unmarked packages. Then, of course, there's the somewhat awkward storage issue; you might consider your local safe-deposit box.

But before getting too carried away with physical gold, it's useful to remember the spring of 1933. An already terrible financial crisis was being capped by a crescendo of banking runs. So on his very first day in office the new president, Franklin Roosevelt, simply closed them. On exactly what authority, it wasn't so clear, so he then asked for and got the Emergency Banking Act. It was passed in such a rush—just like our own 2008 bailout legislation—that the paper trail of precisely what had been legislated was in doubt.

The famous part of the bill did several things: it retroactively approved FDR's bank holiday and provided that only banks approved by the Federal Reserve could thereafter operate; and it enabled the Fed to promise delivery of an unlimited amount of cash to any of those approved banks in order to meet any future run on deposits. That last part, which is exactly what the ECB did to calm runs in Greece, restored everyone's confidence. When the banks did reopen, the lines were back, but this time to deposit instead of withdraw. The stock market had its biggest one-day rally in history.

The not so famous part of the legislation did something else entirely. It enabled the president to issue an executive order confiscating all the privately held gold in the country. And, on April 5, 1933, he did. Here's the order:

POSTMASTER: PLEASE POST IN A CONSPICUOUS PLACE.—JAMES A. FARLEY, Postmaster General

UNDER EXECUTIVE ORDER OF THE PRESIDENT

Issued April 5, 1933

all persons are required to deliver

ON OR BEFORE MAY 1, 1933

all GOLD COIN, GOLD BULLION, AND GOLD CERTIFICATES now owned by them to a Federal Reserve Bank, branch or agency, or to any member bank of the Federal Reserve System.

Executive Order

FORBIDDING THE HOARDING OF GOLD COIN, GOLD BULLION AND GOLD CERTIFICATES

THE WHITE HOUSE,
April 5, 1933.

FRANKLIN D. ROOSEVELT

For Further Information Consult Your Local Bank

GOLD CERTIFICATES may be identified by the words "GOLD CERTIFICATE" appearing thereon. The serial number and the Treasury seal on the face of a GOLD CERTIFICATE are printed in YELLOW. Be careful not to confuse GOLD CERTIFICATES with other issues which are redeemable in gold but which are **not** GOLD CERTIFICATES. Federal Reserve Notes and United States Notes are "redeemable in gold" but are **not** "GOLD CERTIFICATES" and are **not** required to be surrendered

Special attention is directed to the exceptions allowed under Section 2 of the Executive Order

CRIMINAL PENALTIES FOR VIOLATION OF EXECUTIVE ORDER
$10,000 fine or 10 years imprisonment, or both, as provided in Section 9 of the order

Secretary of the Treasury.

The order required citizens to turn in their gold stashes in exchange for $20 of U.S. currency per each ounce of gold. Shortly thereafter, the government raised the price of gold to $35 an ounce, a trade of which even George Soros must be envious.

All in all, a remarkable set of developments, not to be forgotten. It's all well and good to imagine that gold will ultimately constitute a new (old) currency that will supplant paper money. But that will happen only with government consent, not exactly something I'd count on. If you're dedicated to the idea of holding gold through a currency collapse and emerging on the other side with the only viable means of exchange, you might want to go pick up a new toaster—or maybe they give away fondue pots?—by opening an account at a Swiss Canton bank.

Another popular idea is to play gold through the mining companies, and especially the "juniors," the small producers. Many of these hold large gold reserves in the ground but can barely justify pulling it out and processing it (an extremely expensive process, and one that naturally holds down the world gold supply) at current price levels. As a result, their stock is very cheap, but their equity should zoom if gold hits prices that make the extraction profitable.

As an investment thesis, that's not a horrible one. If you are inclined to believe that gold prices are headed for the moon and have the extra capital to make the bet, consider a mutual fund with experienced portfolio managers who can distinguish the good, the bad, and the ugly among the junior miners . . . because there are more of the latter two than the first, I assure you. To be successful in this space, you want to rely on experts to judge management teams, reserves, extraction feasibility and costs, and the like; the passive, mining-focused ETFs can't make those calls.

Meantime, here's a pretty good counterargument about gold: its full glory should have been revealed by now. That is, given the near total meltdown in confidence we suffered in 2007–10; the whir-ring of the central banks' printing presses; and the profligate and unreformed ways of the developed countries' governments . . . why hasn't gold already surpassed its inflation-adjusted highs? Its price topped out in 1980 at about $2,300 per ounce in today's dollars . . . So, despite the pretty good run gold had from a few hundred dol-lars an ounce to somewhere near $2,000 (before falling back), you'd have expected it to do more, no?

The most persuasive argument to me about why gold hasn't yet shone as many expected is a bit provocative: governments haven't yet provided *enough* stimulus. As we noted earlier, perhaps more money will be printed, perhaps much, much more. Many gold bugs say their insurance policy hasn't paid off yet because the real catastrophe still hasn't occurred. But they expect it still will.

Maybe so, maybe not. Certainly, you can't dismiss these argu-ments as silly, as I once did. And since massive inflation is at least a genuine possibility, a bit of insurance doesn't seem like an awful idea.

Timber

The headline here is simple: Harvard has a $3 billion allocation to timber, an enormous 10% of its endowment. After tremendous success in the U.S. woodlands market, buying from paper mills that needed cash and then selling out to other endowments and pension plans who awakened to the value, Harvard headed to Ro-mania and New Zealand and reloaded. It's now stomping around the forests of Brazil, looking for even more.

Timber is special. As mentioned back in chapter 6, it's perhaps the only asset that can do all four portfolio jobs. To the point of this chapter, it is an outstanding inflation hedge that requires little in the way of cap-ex or management. In the last great fight with inflation, 1973 to 1981, timberland outdueled it by an average of about 10% per year. And it has performed well in bear markets for stocks. During the Great Depression, it more than doubled in value, and in 2008 it was up over 9%.

It's also unusual in that it's a real asset that throws off steady income with a modest amount of ongoing effort . . . maybe 6% on average, and that illustrates one of its most unique aspects. Most crops must be harvested and sold in a narrow time window, but if a timber owner doesn't like what he sees out in the world markets, he can always just skip a year of harvesting. The asset just keeps growing, ready for sale when conditions improve. This ability to "store on the stump" provides a level of flexibility that other income-producing assets just don't have—you'll never get back a year of missed rent on an office building.

Moreover, timber is an excellent fundamental way to play the expansion of the world's economies . . . again, without having to invest in local companies and depend on local governments. The Asian markets, in particular, are showing strong demand for wood—a projection by the UN shows timber consumption doubling over the next three decades with, as you can guess, China leading the way. There is also strong worldwide demand for cellulose specialty products, which have a wide range of uses, from pharmaceuticals to paints. So even as newspapers and magazines disappear, the market should continue to expand.

There's also a new and surprising market for wood. Somewhat counterintuitively, "green" regulations are creating a new push toward timber as an energy source. Ever since the EU mandate came down that the continent's utilities would be required to source much of their power from "renewable resources," they've been snooping around the world, looking for sources of cheap wood pellets to burn in their furnaces. Southern soft pine, previously destined to make newspapers, fits the bill.

But the right investment options aren't exactly easy to find. "TIMOs"—timber investment management organizations—are the best way, as they are essentially "registered investment advisors" for timberland. They choose the parcels in the way RIAs pick stocks, sometimes using superior knowledge to buy, for example, acreage that old surveys classify as cheap soft wood but that actually contain stands of more expensive varieties. They diversify portfolios and, each year, make the decision to harvest and sell, or to "store on the stump" and wait for the market to improve.

Unfortunately, most TIMOs focus on institutional investors, though a few do accept smaller accounts, and/or operate private partnerships open to accredited investors. (One group offers direct ownership of ultrarare Hawaiian koa trees, whose wood is prized for musical instruments, but that might be too alternative even for me.) Otherwise, consider a TREIT. These sound like they should be pretty good, and they are: real estate investment trusts that focus on timber. There aren't so many of them, but if you can find one at the right price they are truly lovely diversifiers to a standard portfolio, even one that's holding plenty of traditional real estate. On top of the benefits mentioned above, TREITs typically generate their incomes from a wide variety of buyers all over the world. They deliver a nice "obligor diversification" benefit.

Warning: TREITs are just about the only liquid and practical way to invest in this category. Although there are several ETFs and mutual funds that advertise themselves as timber plays, they are *not* investing in the underlying woodlands; instead, they must be content with investing in companies that own significant timber assets. That's just not the same thing: then you're betting on corporate management and all sorts of financial and stock market conditions that rob the idea of much of its appeal.

Art

Some of those European families who have now preserved their wealth not for a few decades but for several hundred years, describe their formula as "a third, a third, a third": gold, land, and art. Here we are at number three. But for those who didn't grab those Rembrandts when they were new, is art really an investible asset?

Yes. Here's an interesting chart that shows how various classes of art have performed in periods of rising rates, as compared to how stocks have fared.

ART VERSUS EQUITIES IN PERIODS OF RISING INTEREST RATES

Cumulative returns during periods of rising Fed funds rates since 1976

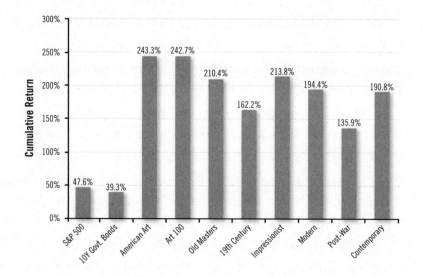

Source: The Collector's Fund

This data is taken from art's very own widely recognized index, the Mei Moses, the existence of which itself is a sign of the normalization of the market. Looking back, it shows that historically significant art outperformed the S&P over the past twenty years while, importantly, displaying a low correlation to it.

The idea of art as an investment class has matured greatly over the past few decades in the United States, but it's been accepted as such in other societies for hundreds of years (at least). There is a powerful cultural reason for this difference: Americans have always trusted their government and economic system. For the rest of the world, having this sort of tangible and portable wealth has long been seen as a necessary protection against unreliable social and financial systems. So if you're feeling just a bit queasy about our societal infrastructure these days . . .

History aside, one big argument for art as an asset class is that it's a globalization play: as the rich get richer and world taste homogenizes, more and more investors are chasing the same, limited class of objects. A related point is that art can serve as a proxy for investment in China, India, and other rapidly developing countries. (This is one reason why the British Rail Pension fund allocated to Chinese ceramics all the way back in the '70s, with excellent results.) History tells us that as cultures gain wealth they inevitably bid up their heritage pieces. Thus, buying recognized (and properly obtained!) art of these cultures is an intriguing way to bet on their continued production of new millionaires and wealthier institutions; you're effectively front-running a predictable trade.

All that said, however, for the non-expert, art investing is beyond tricky. First, of course, is what to buy. Picking among contemporary artists is riskier than choosing among start-ups, and there are profoundly subtle issues that go into choosing among works of even very well known artists. Perhaps you knew that Picasso's paintings from his Marie-Thérèse years are more valuable than his later works, but when a fund manager matter-of-factly mentioned that in passing the other day, it was news to me.

A big part of smart art ownership is working the collection. The value of a piece is largely a consequence of its ownership history, its provenance. That chain of title, from the artist's studio to the present day, shows that the piece is genuine, but it is also improved if the piece has been displayed in great museums, or has been part of important retrospectives of the artist's work. So top owners loan out their pieces to museums and foundations, leading them to be written up in academic and special interest journals, and otherwise promote the pieces as agents do for celebrities.

While art can be an excellent investment, probably more than any other asset class, it's all about the "how." It's not enough to know which pieces may appreciate the most, although that's obviously crucial. You also need access to them as they become available (without having to pay auction house markups or exorbitant dealer commissions); you need to manage their placements; and you need to know when and how to liquidate at a profit.

And, of course, you need to know you're getting the genuine article. New York's prestigious Knoedler Gallery recently collapsed when it fell prey to an elaborate fraud that probably included numerous pieces purchased from a mysterious seller. The jig was up when tests revealed a small "Jackson Pollock" that it had sold for $17 million contained paints that weren't sold until many years after the artist's death. Oops. Probably the best insurance is to rely on an expert whose economic interests are fully aligned with yours.

A few really excellent managers do now run art funds on traditional private equity-type fee structures (one of the most well established funds even lends the acquired art out to investors when it's not parked in museums, creating a combination of investment and time share). One thing to be sure of is that the manager has no conflicts of interest—someone who is a dealer and also runs a fund could easily fall prey to temptation to slide pieces he can't otherwise sell into the fund at an inflated price. Stick with managers who make money only when you do and, where possible, have a proven track record as fiduciaries to investors, not just as art experts.

Art is probably right up there with gold as an inflation hedge, but it can be a lot more enjoyable to live with. And the government has never confiscated Picassos.

Wine, Diamonds, and Other Collectibles

Over centuries, gold and art have proven themselves to be legitimate investment asset classes. But now there's a fund for Stradivarius violins (and cellos!) and a couple for rock star guitars; and others for art deco furniture, rare watches, antique cars, and sports memorabilia. If you happen to be an aficionado, having your hobby double as an investment can make them doubly rewarding, since rare collectibles should do well in an inflationary world. But these aren't for passive investors; the markets are too thin, pricing is unreliable, and middleman markups are killers.

The more interesting questions regard diamonds and wine, two fields attracting a lot of attention (and new funds) lately.

As a real market, wine is farther along. It has something resembling an operating exchange (the Liv-ex), through which real money changes hands at transparent prices, for some of the more famous labels. Impressively, wine recently proved itself to be as legitimate as any other market by hosting its very own bubble: Château Lafite 2009 quickly zoomed to $7,500/case after its release, but then fell 50% over the 2011–12 bear market (darn, should've been in the Latour, which was only down 30%). The NYSE sent along a congratulatory note.

As with art, provenance is absolutely critical. Wine forgeries are a real problem for the obvious reason: there's big money at stake with something that's easy to fake. Copying those labels isn't exactly like duplicating a currency, and the wine inside . . . well, only a few people in the world can really say (and they may not agree!).

And as a long-term store of value . . . well, aging helps only to a point. Your great-grandkids might not enjoy their inheritance all that much.

So, as exotic and fun as wine is, we'll have to take a pass. How about diamonds, which are now attracting attention by ETF sponsors? Aren't they like gold?

Well, no. While they do have the advantage that you can sew them into your clothes, a nifty money-transfer system popular in the Middle Ages, the pricing is beyond opaque. Various attempts to create indexes for diamonds have stumbled because the actual prices at which transactions occur aren't made public.

On a much more basic level, however, here's the issue: diamonds are not fungible. Of the "Four Cs," three—color, cut, and clarity—are quite subjective. And there's an even bigger problem with the fourth.

Carats are indeed standard—200 milligrams, or 100 "points" of 2 milligrams each. The word, by the way, derives from the Greek for carob seed, which was used by the ancients as a standard measure of valuable commodities because of the belief that they all had exactly the same mass. (Nonetheless, smart customers took their own carob seeds to market to protect against merchants who used heavier ones to buy, and lighter ones to sell.) But the 200 milligram standard has been in force globally since 1907, so what's the problem?

It's that two plus two does not equal four in the diamond world. Cut a gold bar in half, and you've just made it more transportable. Cut a diamond in half, and you've destroyed significant value.

So even though all reasonably rare, high-quality real assets should increase in value as paper currencies lose theirs, these very cool collectibles are for connoisseurs, and probably not for disinterested investors.

Real Estate: Sponsor Equity

Well, here's a much less exotic alternative class . . . so much so that some would say it doesn't belong here. True, it hardly bears mentioning that real estate is the most classic inflation hedge of all, or that there exist numerous ways to invest in it already: REITs, REOCs, ETFs, and, of course, direct ownership. But there are in fact some new twists worth knowing about.

Most high net worth investors have extremely indirect access to top-tier real estate operators and their projects, usually only through a byzantine series of feeder, allocator, and funds of funds. The result, too often, has been an enormous total fee load: placement fees, at least one and often two levels of fund fees (the unenviable "double promote"), and then all the implicit fees at the project level: leasing fees, financing fees, and a host of others. At the end of the day, net returns to the investor might easily be 1,000 points less than the gross returns that the project might be producing. In other words, most investors have been taking 25% yield-type risks, but getting paid maybe 15% for the trouble. Nor have they enjoyed the kinds of deal-level co-investment rights that institutional investors enjoy as partial compensation for the fund fees they pay.

All in all, these real estate investments are perhaps not quite as bad as the famous "net points" deals in Hollywood—where even the writer of *Forrest Gump* never saw a penny because it failed to make a "profit"—but they're hardly ideal.

More recently, operators began raising their own funds, rather than depending on the large allocator funds to provide joint venture capital. Investing directly with a bigger operator like this is a major improvement: it might well cut out both placement and one level of fund fees, and still get decent project diversity. But the operator/general will still impose the usual 20% "promote" and drag down total investor returns. Much better, but not perfect.

An even newer and better tasting flavor of private real estate investment is now in the market, called a "sponsor equity" or a "GP co-invest" transaction. The opportunity springs from the fact that many very strong project-level sponsors were dinged badly in the last crash, and their balance sheets haven't recovered.

Many of these sponsors retain commitments from big institutions, like insurance companies and pension plans, to fund big projects as limited partners—but they don't have the necessary liquidity to make good on their own capital commitments as general partners to those partnerships. As a result, they're willing to share their generous GP economics with new investors who can commit the necessary long-term capital. This is a rare case, the only instance in the entire book, in which outside investors can be the beneficiaries, instead of the victims, of the 20% promote so common in investment partnerships.

These transactions are probably as close as an outside investor will ever get to the economics that are the reason real estate insiders play the game, and are certainly infinitely better—from a fee point of view—than the old allocator fund model. Those may still provide the comfort of famous financial institution brand names, but that's an awfully expensive luxury. A well-chosen sponsor equity transaction has radically higher odds of generating real upside.

While we're on the subject, spare a moment for a quick word on some megatrends shaping tomorrow's real estate market. Falling real income, boomerang kids, longer lives, and higher energy costs point to one thing: increasing population density. There is every reason to think that the future will look like the past: families filling different levels of multigenerational housing. It's already happening: Pew Research says that the number of twenty-five- to thirty-four-year-olds living with their parents has doubled over the past three decades and is now up to 20%. Communities will be drawn together, quite literally, by the lower costs of sharing infrastructure and energy delivery. Fewer people will be able to afford the luxuries of large stand-alone homes, large yards, and expensive commutes.

Another factor driving things in the same direction is the emerging "many hats" economy. As the number of full-time jobs continues to shrink, more and more people will wear many hats, pursuing two or three moneymaking activities at the same time. That increases the need for common, technology-enabled work spaces, and it reduces demand for dedicated office campuses. And a more entrepreneurial society thrives on random physical interactions of like-purposed individuals, as in Silicon Valley, and now Manhattan. There is a reason that the overwhelming percentage of innovation comes out of densely populated areas.

Many operators are specialists in projects that will take advantage of trends like these: multigenerational housing, apartment complexes with shared workspaces, urban shopping. If you can jump in via a sponsor equity–type deal, you'll be playing a big trend cheek by jowl with the cognoscenti.

Infrastructure

If there's one sure bet for a worldwide growth category, here it is. Tens of trillions will be spent on infrastructure around the globe over the next few decades on projects from new energy plants to hospitals in developing countries ("greenfield" projects), and on reconstruction of failing bridges and tunnels in developed ones ("brownfield"). On this point, by the way, the United States currently ranks an embarrassing twenty-fourth on the global infrastructure quality list.

The latest wave of these projects are "P3s," public private partnerships. As the great robber barons would tell you, monopolies can be awesome investments; but, annoyingly, legal ones can be tough to find these days. P3s are not merely legal; they're actually government sponsored. The new Jordan Bridge, in South Hampton Roads, Virginia, is a prime example.

Its predecessor was a crumbling 1928 lift bridge that the town fathers closed in 2008, even though they knew they couldn't even afford demolition, much less repair. They sold it to a private consortium for $10, with just a few conditions attached, like the obligation to build a new one. Today a spectacular new one-mile span stands in its place, tall enough for ships to pass under, no lift required. The residents have to pay nearly $2 to cross it, instead of the old fifty cents, but otherwise not a penny of taxpayer money was involved. (Including when a construction accident and other problems increased completion time and budget: the private owners bore the risk.)

But purely private deals are the biggest part of the market, and may provide investors better returns. Opportunities are expanding especially rapidly in energy production, from hydrocarbon extraction to generation to transportation. A key reason is shocking advances in drilling technologies, which are unleashing a wave of oil and gas extraction likely to make the United States the world leader in both categories in a few years. That implies vast new construction. And simultaneously, states are deregulating their electric utilities, opening the way for privately financed power generation facilities.

Those have shown some spectacular returns; some specialist funds in this space have produced 3x gross returns and 30% IRRs over the course of many years running. In fact, demand for operating electric plants is so high—among retail electric providers as well as MLPs—that active bidding for them breaks out; one large energy plant construction project recently produced a 1,000% return over the course of a single year for that reason. That was an outlier, but aggressive firms in this field will almost certainly see many other situations with unusual risk/reward ratios.

Outside the United States, many smart folks believe infrastructure is the very best way to profit from the developing economies—China in particular. Immature economies will experience fits and starts as they adjust to true capitalism and a free-market world, and their equity markets could be just too much of a roller coaster. Long-term infrastructure projects might be a surer bet.

In choosing among infrastructure projects, it's fair to say that water and energy–type projects are probably safer than transportation-related deals, simply because they tend to have less exposure to the ups and downs of economies over time. In addition, most utilities are already well set up to pass along inflation and higher operating expenses to their users through recurring billing.

What isn't so interesting? Projects that depend on major ongoing tax subsidies to produce returns. Hoping that taxpayers will continue to fund projects that would otherwise not be viable—the wind industry in the United States is a prime example—can lead to some very ugly consequences.

The most direct way to participate in these projects is through one of numerous private infrastructure funds that focus on the space, typically sponsored by the usual global brand names. (Macquarie, the Australian investment bank, is possibly the leader in the space, but Goldman, Citi, Morgan Stanley, and the other big U.S. institutions are also major participants.) As noted, however, some smaller specialist funds can be great ways to participate, especially in the energy field. A few mutual funds also specialize in publicly traded entities that benefit from the trend to greater privatization of traditionally governmental building projects, and these have held up pretty well amid market downturns, probably due to the stability of the underlying projects. Finally, you can also simply purchase municipal bonds that are backed by fees from specific projects.

TIPS

We've already acknowledged that Treasury Inflation Protected Securities, as a financial instrument, keep odd company by hanging around with all the physical assets in this chapter. But you'll remember why: they are perhaps the best in the world for preserving purchasing power . . . if you buy them the right way.

The principal amount of a TIPS bond adjusts on an annual

basis along with changes in the CPI, but the coupon rate stays the same. So if there's inflation, the face amount of the bond goes up, and you're paid more interest as a result (the same rate, but higher face value). And, of course, you get that greater amount at maturity. So the inflation protection is excellent.

You may also recall the claim that TIPS might be the most unique investment in the world, and now we'll spill the beans on why that's so. They are truly a no-lose bet, because that principal will not *decrease* below the original face amount in the case of deflation. You'd naturally expect the inflation reset feature to work in both directions, so that if inflation were negative, the principal due at maturity would decline. But that is not the case; the principal never goes below the original face amount. Heads you win, tails you don't lose—and therefore, amid deflation, win again.

Maybe that doesn't strike you as so amazing at first. Recall that a regular bond is a loser in an inflationary period, but a big winner in a deflationary period . . . having a fixed amount of money owed to you as prices fall means your purchasing power keeps increasing. So: with regular bonds you'll do well if we do fall into a Japan-style deflationary spiral, but lose your shirt if inflation roars back. With TIPS, it's heads you win; tails, same result.

Although you can purchase TIPS through mutual funds and ETFs, direct ownership is preferable. TIPS are long-dated assets, and that makes them volatile (despite the principal adjustment feature) if interest rates move a lot. By owning them through a fund without a redemption date, therefore, you could lose, but if you hold a TIPS directly, that's not a problem . . . just hold to maturity. Note carefully that huge difference: "just hold to maturity" advice works great for TIPS, but *not*, as we've noted before, for regular bonds. With TIPS (only), the principal amount increases to protect your purchase power at maturity.

When you buy, buy new ones. If you're purchasing in the aftermarket, the principal adjustment mechanism may have already kicked in, and then a deflationary spurt could push it back down to the original face amount. And hold them in your IRA if possible . . . they do throw off current tax when that principal amount readjusts.

Water

All evidence seems to indicate that people really do enjoy water. Too bad, because only about 1% of it on the entire planet is potable.

You already know that the supply is under incredible and growing pressure from increasing populations. The exact reason that's true, however, is a bit surprising. It's not so much that more people drink more water, or even use it for other purposes like bathing. It's that as the demand for protein food sources increases, the need for fresh water to create it explodes: from this point of view, in fact, eating a hamburger is the same as taking a twelve-hour shower.

Nor is there an obvious technology answer. Desalinization is extremely energy intensive—some estimates have Saudi Arabia utilizing 40% of its domestic oil usage for the purpose.

In the United States, folks may well first feel the pinch not from a lack of water in the taps, but rather from disruptions in electricity production and transportation. The Hoover Dam may soon have to shut down because of low water levels in Lake Mead, and the Tennessee Valley Authority has ongoing issues with operating its generators as a result of high water temperatures (a function of both drought and extreme heat). Even scarier, stretches of the mighty Mississippi, a main artery in the nation's economy, are under threat of shutdown from simple lack of depth.

The world does indeed face an incredibly serious water shortage. But whereas it's easy to invest in water-related businesses, it's hard to invest in water itself. And mostly, even where you can, you're really buying into a transportation business.

This was highlighted during a recent investor pitch by the owners of an enormous and incredible source of wonderful fresh water, a melting glacier (no kidding). It sits at ocean's edge in Chile, where, thanks to Milton Friedman's participation in drafting the constitution, private ownership of such resources is possible. Investors, puzzled about the delivery to thirsty jurisdictions, were assured that the issue would be addressed by cutting-edge "VLB" technology. A nervous silence followed, but eventually someone asked the inevitable. And then all was revealed: the idea, under development for many years, was to employ tugboats pulling "very large bags." Oh.

With that caution, here are some ideas for the ultimate liquid investment.

In the private placement arena, several "green" venture firms are pursuing water-specific solutions. Of course, any major improvement in desalination or recycling technologies should find an enormous market. (One respected group is funding, really truly, the construction of a gigantic mountaintop dehumidifier that will take water from the air, clean it, and release it into pipes to the valley below.) But an even more promising area may be more efficient irrigation systems; approximately 70% of fresh water is used in agriculture, so that's where modest improvements could drive enormous consequences.

On the PE side, water-related businesses, like treatment facilities and equipment providers, are promising targets for roll-ups;

the current industry is so fractured that some consolidation is inevitable.

A very few private funds do specialize in direct ownership of water rights, including riparian right ownership in the United States (to get these, one buys land to which the rights attach), water resource rights in Australia (one of the more progressive jurisdictions for water rights), and maybe even that glacier. Firms like these are probably the best "pure plays" available.

But overall, water investing options remain underdeveloped. The obvious one is a water ETF, but as with timber, this actually invests in listed companies in the industry, and not in the commodity itself; it is also small and has failed to deliver positive results since inception. There are also a handful of unit investment trusts that specialize in water-related investments, but these, too, are focused on operating companies. Another possibility is publicly traded water utilities (there are a couple dozen worldwide), although they tend to produce exactly what you'd expect: utility-type returns that do not capture the unique water value proposition. You can find a few public companies that have significant water resources, typically as a by-product of their main businesses (forest products or resorts ownership, for example). At the end of the day, for U.S. investors looking for traded water securities, the most direct method is probably municipal bonds tied to specific water projects.

There are also three established exchanges around the world (in the U.S. Southwest, Australia, and Chile), but nobody has figured out how to scale these local water rights markets to the broader investment universe.

Innovation is on the way, however. A new water index is in the works that should allow investors to invest directly in the commodity, and will also permit utilities and industrials to hedge out the risks of rising water costs. Several new financial instruments, not dissimilar to cat bonds and weather derivatives, are also on the drawing boards. Keep an eye out for new opportunities; water has the single best long-term investment thesis on the planet.

In Review

Gold is, of course, the classic in this field, but how and how much are tricky issues. Gold ETFs are the obvious way to invest and should be fine in moderate inflation, but many gold bugs prefer to hold physical gold; and the truly paranoid hold it overseas.

Art has more of a track record as wealth insurance than many Americans appreciate. The issues are in the buying: the right pieces, at the right prices, in the right ways. For non-experts, pursuing it as an investment, going through a fund with a great manager, is the best bet.

Timber is in a class by itself. Both the income stream it throws off and the land's residual value increase with inflation; it is the ultimate renewable; it's an excellent bet on worldwide economic development; and maintenance is minimal.

TIPS are the only financial asset that double as "real." And they feature a spectacular asymmetry, increasing in value in inflationary periods, but not decreasing below the issue price with deflation.

Diamonds and wine sure are fun to think about as investments, but they don't quite make the grade. Wine is subject to spoilage and easy forgery, and diamonds aren't fungible.

Real estate "sponsor equity" or "GP co-invest deals" dramatically improve the attraction of this class of private investment, which historically has been very fee-intensive and somewhat skewed against passive investors.

Infrastructure investment is a long-term play that should provide rising revenues from user fees and taxes, both domestically and internationally. Utility-style projects are probably more reliable wealth protectors than transportation-related transactions.

Finally, water is the ultimate long-term play, but direct ownership is extremely difficult. As its true costs become more apparent, so will the economic consequences of reducing waste; one idea is to invest in technologies that promote more efficient use of the fresh water we already have.

Final Thoughts

Inflation is not certain, but it is likely. Sovereign credit risk is real. And the soundness of the financial system is not beyond question. Those three are powerful arguments for allocating some portion of your portfolio to the assets described in this chapter.

For average investors, TIPS (bought properly, as described) are as close to a no-lose bet as you'll find on this earth. And for the wealthier, direct timber ownership is close behind.

CHAPTER 9

....

The Big Picture

If you can look into the seeds of time,
And say which grain will grow and which will not,
Speak then to me . . .
　　　—Banquo, *Macbeth*, Act I, Scene 3

Don't you hate it when you're looking over a too-huge menu, ask the waiter for recommendations, and he helpfully replies, "Everything here is good"?

We're going to try to be a bit more constructive. The previous four chapters suggested strategies for the main four investment jobs, an à la carte approach. Here we'll step it up a notch and talk about combining investments into a lovely, complete dinner—a panoramic, risk-tolerant portfolio.

As you know, the thinking about portfolio construction has evolved very far from the old 60/40 approach. The big advance was the endowment model, also called "strategic asset allocation," based on modern portfolio theory. As you also know, the crash then required some, shall we say, um, fine-tuning—placing a new focus on strategies that perform well in crises, and on previously unnoticed common vulnerabilities among assets and strategies.

The "jobs"-based approach of the previous four chapters is a great start against this background; a portfolio comprised of a mix of investments from them should provide what folks in the computer security industry would call PGP: pretty good protection. In this chapter, though, we'll take a deeper dive into portfolio allocation.

Pretty obviously, those four jobs happen to align with increasing levels of wealth. Starting investors would typically focus on income and risk reduction; wealthier ones will allocate more heavily toward return enhancement and purchase power protection.

Beyond that, we can (and should!) get fancier. And so we'll describe some specific combinations of alternative investments that might work well for investors of different means, and which should contribute to that "risk-tolerant" portfolio through non-correlation, active risk management, and absolute diversification.

This chapter also introduces two new concepts into the dialogue about panoramic portfolio construction. The first is something called the "liquidity ratio." Many of the best opportunities are not available in liquid form, and liquidity premiums are high these days; when prudent to do so, they should be captured. To help an investor understand when that might be—when he may be erring on the side of too much liquidity, as some might be these days—we'll propose a simple rule of thumb.

Secondly, for the more adventurous, we'll also spend some time on adding an "overlay": weighting the portfolio to maximize performance under various plausible economic "regimes" that we may see over the next many years.

Liquidity, Reprised

We've already discussed the central role of liquidity in individual allocation decisions. Needless to say, everyone must remain fully prepared for upcoming lifestyle expenses, potential emergencies, and the like. Beyond the obvious issues, the question really depends as much on psychology and personality as anything else.

Moreover, cash itself is an investment. The old-fashioned way to wealth is, indeed, to buy when the blood is running in the streets. (Although, sadly, as far as I can tell, neither any of the oft-quoted Rothschilds nor John D. Rockefeller actually ever said that . . . no worries, they should have.) Having cash at the ready when others must liquidate at any price is probably the single greatest moneymaking trick in history. Keeping plenty of the green stuff around is an example of the "level theory," which holds that idiots and geniuses frequently do the same things, but for very different reasons. Allocating to cash is, indeed, very sophisticated.

That said, some high-net-worth investors' holdings put them, pretty obviously, beyond both safe and prepared-for opportunity, and probably right over the line into "just missing out." That's the line the liquidity ratio is meant to define.

The calculation is simple. Net worth, in millions, is the numerator. The denominator is the *greater* of: 1, or the investor's "burn rate"—the amount, in millions, by which his current annual expenditures exceed current income. So, if income exceeds expenses, stick with 1. Thus, an investor with a $3 million net worth who's got a net annual spend of $500,000 has a liquidity ratio of 3 (three over one). An investor with $20 million net worth, who's spending $3 million a year on lifestyle and has $1 million salary, has a LR of 10 (twenty over two).*

---

* Naturally, many wealthier clients are anchored in certain kinds of investments because of their own businesses or the source of their existing net worth; or they have predictable, large liquidity needs on the horizon. Such personal circumstances obviously have to be taken into account in this analysis.

OK. Then, the rule of thumb is: investors with a liquidity ratio of less than 2 should stick with cash and liquid alternatives, and within the Starter Menu below.

Investors with an LR of 2 or 3 can consider adding some non-liquid investments. The suggestion is to multiply the liquidity ratio by 10% to get a target budget. That is, someone with a liquidity ratio of 3 could have 30% of his investment portfolio in semi- and illiquid strategies (your primary residence is not part of your portfolio for this purpose; other properties are). The Intermediate Menu has some suggestions for you.

Investors with an LR of 4 or more should almost certainly be adding more illiquid investments, grabbing some meat and potatoes from the Advanced Menu. Since cash is such a powerful asset in crisis periods, there's no point in going crazy, and my own suggestion would be, except for the ultrawealthy, to limit illiquid strategies to 50% of net worth.

Sample Menus

OK, you know I have to say this: very obviously, *these ideas are simply offered as rough general suggestions, and certainly not as specific advice for any particular investor.* But they're a decent place from which to start thinking about allocation strategies. After all, we all hate boring waiters.

Sample Starter Menu

Job 1 (income): MLPs, multiasset ETFs, EM debt mutual funds, royalty trusts, BDCs, Floaters (30%)

Job 2 (risk reducers): smart beta and multi-alternative mutual funds, TREITs, and cash (35%)

Job 3 (return enhancers): long-only U.S. stocks; global blue chips (25%)

Job 4 (purchase power protection): TIPS (10%)

(NOTE: As discussed, TIPS actually perform multiple jobs, so they not only reduce risk but also produce income. Also, be mindful of the *total* equity exposure—smart beta funds will decline in a crash, just not as much as long-only stock positions.)

Sample Intermediate Menu

Add to the previous holdings, with increases to Jobs 2 and 3 total allocations as appropriate:

Job 1: peer-to-peer lending; privately placed royalties; mezz debt

Job 2: funds of hedge funds; managed futures mutual funds; short bias funds

Job 3: global macro hedge funds; venture funds; distressed and activist hedge funds; O&G partnerships

Job 4: Sponsor equity RE; gold ETFs; art funds

Sample Advanced Menu

Add to the previous holdings, with increases to Jobs 3 and 4 total allocations as appropriate:

Job 1: cat bonds; micro PE

Job 2: Relative value equity and credit hedge funds; arbitrage hedge funds; CTAs; farmland funds

Job 3: angel investing; PE secondary and growth; EM hedge funds & FoFs

Job 4: direct timber and art ownership; physical gold; infrastructure

These portfolios may be great long-term targets, but we're nothing if not practical. So, for those deeply immersed in the 60/40 world, how do we get from here to there?

The top priority for most investors is getting away from the extreme interest risk of traditional bond funds. I'd suggest moving out of those and into the liquid alternative income investments from chapter 5, along with TREITs and TIPS. Meanwhile, if you're holding specific bonds and want to hold them to maturity, that's made safer by pairing them with some gold ETFs: "gold/ bond" sounds like a 007 title, but here the mission is to protect your purchasing power.

On the equity side, the suggestion is to first limit volatility by rotating long-only holdings of traditional mutual funds and ETFs into long/short, multi-alternative, and managed futures mutual funds.

Now, that could be enough to get you going. But there are also other, more sophisticated, issues that go into creating an optimal overall portfolio: some focus further on risk reduction, and others relate to the bigger picture economic scenarios that may play out over the next several years . . . and which could have enormous implications for your holdings.

Risk-Tolerant Portfolios, Continued . . .

Following the above allocation blueprints should indeed provide a panoramic portfolio that will serve most people well in most circumstances. But it's impossible to pay too much attention to risk-tolerance. Beyond the active risk management introduced with hedging strategies, it's always wise to step back and consider how much of a portfolio is comprised of "uncorrelated" strategies and how well it is "absolutely diversified."

To recap, diversification has been well understood as a fundamental tool of risk reduction since . . . well, at least King Solomon, given the quote that kicks this book off. Neither he nor the modern portfolio theorists were wrong about that, but in 2008 the world's growing complexities overcame the power of relatively narrow diversification tactics.

In the postmortem of that crash, there were a few big realizations. One, discussed in chapter 4, was overreliance on convergent strategies, such as classic relative value, distressed investing, and other strategies that assume prices will "converge" to an inherent value or historical relationship over time.

When markets go haywire, divergent strategies can be the ones that rescue the portfolio from a major overall drawdown. These depend much more on top-down, big picture–type analyses rather than any sort of intrinsic valuations; after all, when panic hits, no one cares what prices "should" be. Good global macro managers, who can play the world's trends with ultra-liquid futures contracts, tend to be the nimble winners at times like those. Other managed futures strategies can perform well, too, and so can volatility arbitrage, currency, high-frequency managers, and several niche strategies that operate on basic supply-demand dynamics. Creating a portfolio of genuinely uncorrelated income streams is tough to do without including some divergent strategies like these.

And another big lesson was that allocators had failed to recognize how a single factor could bring down so many strategies in one fell swoop. In attempting to avoid a repeat, investors and advisors should shoot for "absolute diversification." One should, for example, constantly evaluate how much of the overall portfolio is subject to direct and indirect U.S. stock market risk. Prior to the crash, many institutions had been thinking their "absolute return" buckets, like merger and convertible arbitrage, were diversifying their normal equity allocations. Not so, of course. And on that subject, it's important to recall that the world's markets are more heavily "coupled" than ever before; so a stock market collapse in one part of the world is likely to be felt in most markets at the same time.

An underappreciated aspect of absolute diversification concerns who, exactly, is on the hook for the payment streams that constitute the income portion of the portfolio (known as "counterparty risk"). Of course single-obligor bonds raise obvious credit risk issues, but often investors don't think enough about diversifying the type and geographic location of the obligors in a portfolio. Adding, for example, pharmaceutical royalties in lieu of yet another pile of typical corporate bonds provides a non-obvious but extremely useful kind of diversification to a portfolio; even if corporate issuers get in trouble in a slow economy, people are likely to keep buying their meds.

Reaching for absolute diversification also requires monitoring exposure to duration and credit exposure, as well as sovereign, currency, and inflation risks (to name a few!). But perhaps the single biggest vulnerability to guard against is reliance on strategies that themselves are heavily leveraged. Big corporate buyout deals, real estate developments, and credit arbitrage strategies can fail together despite their apparent diversity. It's not just how much leverage the investor is using; it's also about how much leverage the investments are using. That's why, among the illiquid strategies, the lower leverage ones like venture, growth PE, and real assets are so important.

Of course, the need for uncorrelated strategies and absolute diversification largely grows from the fact that there's so much big-picture macro stuff going on out there. It would be a lovely thing if we could assemble one portfolio that performed equally well under every possible set of financial conditions, or what the academics call "regimes." The goal of this book is to suggest portfolio constructions that mitigate against the unforeseen as much as possible, but the fact is that different, plausible economic environments will certainly have profound influences on different kinds of investments.

So let's take a quick look into that crystal ball.

The Overlay

Overlay is a favorite word in the alternatives world, and like many others, it can have different meanings. Here, we're using the slang for "economic worldview." If you have strong feelings about where things might go from here, or special vulnerabilities to worry about, you might well tilt your investments accordingly.

So if you're dead certain that inflation will run wild over the next many years, ignore all previous advice, pile on the maximum possible leverage (at today's ultra low fixed rates, of course), and buy depressed real assets. If you think all-out depression is ahead, sell everything else and go all in on quality bonds. If you're not so sure, keep reading.

We'll look at three big-picture economic "regimes," and some of the systemic risks that are lurking out there, to see how they might impact the balance of a portfolio.

Deflation?

We've discussed the fact that the world's central bankers are desperate to see a little inflation right now. That would solve a lot of problems, including the huge economic albatross of U.S. homes with values less than their mortgages. And normally, you would think that a dedicated effort by the central banks, with the collusion of elected officials who see inflation as a painless way out of their obligations to creditors and social program recipients, would be unstoppable. Inflation should prevail.

But . . . not so fast. The Fed has held rates near zero for five years (as of this writing); perhaps you can give it credit for avoiding a repeat of the '30s, at least so far, but it is also possible that the lack of real economic growth in the face of all that stimulus just means we've delayed the inevitable.

Here's an even scarier idea. Maybe the bond market has figured out that the end of systemic risk means: the advent of systemic risk. Surely one reason Treasury bond rates have been so low is pure fear . . . investors have taken haven in U.S. government obligations. So, as the world begins to solve our problems and get out of the woods, what happens? Rates creep up. But just a 2% or 3% increase in rates would fairly quickly add hundreds of billions of new interest rate costs to the deficit, in principle calling for more austerity and hence deflationary pressure. Ugh.

Meantime, don't forget two other deflationary superheroes capable of a good fight even against the mighty Central Bankers' Alliance, and which are completely unrelated to that debt overhang. They're strong already, and gaining power all the time.

One is demographics. You may know that Japan suffered an 80% decline in stock and real estate prices over the past two decades, and that the Nikkei is still two-thirds lower than its peak.

A history note for you youngsters out there: right before their bubble burst, many Americans had conceded the title of World's Greatest Economy to that small island. The Japanese were vacuuming up American landmarks, from Rockefeller Center to the Pebble Beach golf course, causing a nationalistic recoil. The yen was sure to be king, and the dollar was headed to the dustbin as the world's reserve currency.

Then, the next twenty years happened. They revealed the power of a real estate bubble, too much debt, and a very rapidly aging population. Hmmm . . .

That terrible tale is worth remembering when considering the possibility of deflation here and in Western Europe. There are, of course, many reasons why other developed nations are not like Japan, but there are also enough similarities to make you nervous. Europe is almost as old, with declining average productivity, negative birth rates, lots of debt, and, in some countries, a lingering real estate bubble. America, too, is graying rapidly but at least has a positive net population growth rate, pushed just north of zero by immigration.

But the scary one is China. Its demographics are about to step into an open elevator shaft, a rapid aging accelerated by the consequences of that one-child policy.

So that's one half of the Deflation Duo. The other is even more pernicious, because everyone's urging it on: technology. Perhaps the very fact that it's so obvious has made this issue hard to see. Capitalism always seeks efficiency, of course, but it now has the ultimate enabler working as its partner. The consequence is an accelerating wave of job destruction.

Yes, yes, I know: from at least the time of steam engines people have wailed that technology would destroy jobs. It never has. Instead, it's always created new kinds. Leading economists today pooh-pooh the idea that technology is the Shiva of jobs because of that wolf-crying past. But I think we've reached a tipping point.

You've no doubt heard about the famous technology rule of thumb called Moore's Law. Gordon Moore predicted in 1965 that the processing power of a microprocessor would double every eighteen months or so, and that has turned out to be weirdly accurate over the subsequent decades. On further analysis, however, it appears that the "power curve" of technology has been operating for a very long time indeed . . . according to Ray Kurzweil, since the dawn of history.

Now the very interesting thing about an exponential curve is that it actually looks and feels gradual for a very long time, barely different from a normal arithmetic curve. But watch out: when the turn comes, it forms an elbow and shoots nearly straight up. And that, I think, is where we are now.

You're perfectly well aware that the advances so far have destroyed whole categories of what used to be middle-class careers, but, truly, we're just getting started: because here come the robots. Some already clean gutters and vacuum homes; many are deployed in smart manufacturing plants; and now the most sophisticated surgeries, through the smallest incisions, are performed with the help of C3PO's cousins. Can broad destruction of labor-based jobs really lie so far ahead?

But even those disruptions may be dwarfed as today's simple 3D printing evolves into full-blown digital fabrication. Simple devices like guns are already producible out of thin air from a machine the size of an aquarium. What lies ahead is production of working electronics right out of the machine and assembly of proteins to create human organs on demand. If you thought it was hilarious that George Jetson could arrive home from work, select a dinner off a menu from something that looked like a microwave, and have it magically appear, laugh no longer: protein spray with a little flavoring and coloring has already made food printing a reality. The implications for every supply chain, from production to distribution to sale, are impossible to fathom. Welcome to the post-scarcity economy.

Technology efficiencies have always been thought of as a "good" source of deflation, and perhaps they are. But tell that to the displaced workers' army that is likely to be created by what Kurzweil calls the law of accelerating returns.

And So?

In a deflationary period, the most valuable assets to hold are high-quality fixed-rate bonds, the longer term the better. So if that's where we're headed, end of discussion.

But that really is an enormous gamble: if inflation does manage to take off, exactly those bonds will be among the hardest hit assets. So, it might be time to play chess here. Why make a one-way bet when you can make a multipurpose move?

There are, in fact, a few (very few, but still, that's better than zero) investments that should do well in both inflationary and deflationary environments. We've already mentioned three explicitly. TIPS are the top choice for wealth preservation; they should work out in almost any realistic economic environment. A second one is timber, our favorite real asset. And a third is a control position in companies that provide essential goods and services.

Together, that's the somewhat obvious all-weather trifecta. But there are more subtle and intriguing ideas, too.

The first is developable raw land in great locations. The inflation story on that is clear, but how this asset works in deflationary periods isn't so obvious. For a clue, imagine the New York skyline . . . and remember that its most classic structure, the Empire State Building, was erected in the depths of the Great Depression.

"Why" is a fun one to ponder; take a second. It's because: although the raw land value did fall, the cost of developing fell far faster. The materials, the architectural fees, the site labor, all got very cheap, very fast. A very similar scenario could play out again. Eventually the government will take whatever action is necessary to force reflation (see below), and then that building becomes extraordinarily more valuable than its cost.

In chapter 7, we talked about some trends that will change real estate consumption, very likely toward greater density. That would imply that one excellent longer term strategy is to hold developable properties near town centers. Properties that can draw some income against relatively low operating expenses are extra attractive; urban parking lots are ideal examples. Then you've got a fantastic long-term option, and when the time is right the property can be sold or developed.

Just don't forget to hold the land at very low carrying costs. Deflation would be a complete disaster for strategies involving high, long-term leverage against fixed assets.

In an analogously odd way, gold also has obvious appeal amid inflation, and hidden appeal during deflation. Look again at the Great Depression, and recall that gold prices rose hugely. Yes, it's because the government was officially setting prices, which it can't do quite as easily now, but if the Fed were to announce tomorrow that it was a buyer of gold at $5,000 an ounce, that would become the metal's new price.

Many smart people (like my partner Jim Rickards) think that gold is the reflation tool of last resort, because it can't fight back. Other countries can competitively devalue the currencies when we do; gold can't do a thing. But once gold is repriced, everything else is likely to follow. And in that scenario, gold becomes a deflation play, not just an inflation hedge.

More Directionless Volatility?

Inertia applies to economies just as it does in the physics lab. So you certainly have to consider that the next few years might look a lot like the last few: very low growth and lots of "directionless volatility." A slow deleveraging process grinds along; Europe very gradually reforms into a more centralized union; China begrudgingly dribbles out assistance to the rest of the world because it has to maintain its export economy to prevent civil unrest.

Although the accompanying fits and starts generate volatility, there's no overall up or down direction to it; and it is magnified in the equity markets, and muted in the credit markets, by excess but underutilized liquidity.

Which is one key to understanding the opportunities. Illiquidity premiums are very high right now, but one can imagine that, over time, all that extra cash in the system will do as the Fed hopes, and leak out into risk assets. Even if not, so long as there's no real disaster, then capturing the extra return that more illiquid investments offer will have looked very smart. Many funds and specific projects, from real estate to infrastructure, are willing to accept better investor terms than has been typical, while the underlying projects simultaneously offer better returns because of lesser competition.

One underappreciated facet of a muddling-along environment is how much the demand for top quality income securities will grow (thus depressing their yields).

There are two reasons: the first is that, as the population ages, there is greater and greater demand for income . . . and fewer products, at higher prices, to satisfy that hunger. The second is that regulators are increasingly demanding higher levels of better quality collateral to stand behind loans and derivatives.

So, how does more of the same map over to investment choices?

Low net exposure long/short stocks strategies should be able to withstand sudden swings in the market. At the same time, they also function like bond funds, cranking out small gains month after month (at least if you find the right manager!), but without the interest rate risk. Conversely, programmatic managed futures trading, such as many managed futures strategies employ, can have problems. Trends don't stick around long enough to generate big profits, and trading expenses mount very quickly.

Income products that have only modest exposure to rising rates (because we can't risk being wrong on that one) are interesting, including MLPs and the various royalty investments we've mentioned. Quality emerging market bonds will provide more income than those from developed countries and should gain value over time as: (1) demand for superior financial assets grows; (2) their societies stabilize; and (3) rates around the world harmonize.

Serious start-ups (translation: not social media) can do well in these periods because the uncertainty drives larger firms to reduce internal R & D expenditures, making them turn to acquisitions for innovation. And, by the way, engineering-heavy ventures have a wonderful emergency exit if their model fails. "Acqui-hires" are a primary source of recruiting for the giant technology outfits . . . computer science talent is in dreadfully short supply, so small companies that are full of quality geeks often get purchased just for their teams. There aren't many chances to practice "risk adjusted" venture investing, but that's one.

And lastly, here's a huge "tell" about what the hedge fund world itself expects the best kinds of hedge fund strategies to be over the next few years: they're hiring macroeconomists like crazy, while fundamental analysts' résumés pile up. That points to a belief that governmental policies will continue to dominate the world financial system. Chalk one up for global macro.

Inflation?

All that having been said, let's repeat: inflation is the biggest threat we face.

The point's been made and we won't belabor it, so let's just toss in one more simple fun fact: over the next twenty-five years, the graying of America will push Medicare and Social Security payments, by themselves, to 16% of GDP. But the *total* deficit over the past forty years, including defense spending and all other social programs, has averaged only 18.5% of GDP. In the absence of huge economic growth, which is awfully hard to see, that's just one more reason, along with the many previously articulated, that the inflation scenario is the front-runner.

Can the Fed keep it under control? Well, if tech keeps eating the jobs market, so the real economy never regains full steam, and inflation rears anyway because of the number of dollars racing around the system, what will the Fed do about it? It can choose between: (1) smothering a sputtering recovery, risking deflation, and possibly even driving social unrest; or (2) letting inflation drive down the real indebtedness of the population, elevate home prices, and hurt the small percentage of the population that are savers. I bet on that one.

If that's the way it goes, what strategies should we favor?

Modest inflation is OK for the stock market. So in a "smart beta" strategy, you would favor managers who have bigger "net long" positions. As for credit instruments, both distressed debt and high yield should do well, as the liquidity flood reduces borrower stress. Whatever else, avoid fixed income, and pile into the flexible-return stream vehicles described in chapter 5. And look again at peer-to-peer lending, with its higher returns and low-duration risk.

Of course, the real assets should be the real stars, and all those chapter 8 investments should perform well. In addition, those same private equity strategies that look so scary in a deflationary period might make you look like a genius in this scenario: the assets will soar in value, and multiples will expand, while the debt remains fixed. For the same reason that the housing market would benefit hugely, so would leveraged buyouts.

What about hyperinflation, a scary but real issue? In that scenario the best single bet is owning big chunks of operating, cash-flowing businesses that sell things people need to buy. At the start of Weimar Germany's hyperinflation of 1921 and 1922, many German investors were initially not so alarmed, because the stock market was doing very well . . . it was keeping pace by increasing in value in local currency terms. But eventually, of course, the money itself became worthless. Among the few who survived in reasonable shape were the business owners, who controlled the factories and bakeries, and who could trade and barter until the new monetary system went into place. Yes, I know it all sounds a bit extreme, but for this particular thought experiment, that's not a crazy precedent.

Systemic Risks

Now, I hate to be an alarmist, but it really is important to get a grip on just how big the systemic risks are right now. That has everything to do with how much you might want to entrust to the financial system, and how much leverage and illiquidity risk you can take. We're not talking here about the "regimes" as we did above; now the question is: how serious a threat is another sudden and genuine crisis?

One measure is the size of the derivatives market, the shadowy world of interest rate, currency, credit default, and total return swaps . . . and an army of similar nonstandardized, poorly understood instruments. Banks, hedge funds, insurance companies, and all other financial institutions now issue and buy these in unimaginable bulk. The big, big issue with them is not their terms; it's that they aren't recorded anywhere, so in a crisis you can't guess who is holding which set of hot potatoes. That means you don't know who might fail; and if you don't know that, you won't do business with anybody. That was a primary reason why the credit markets ceased to function in 2008. No wonder Warren Buffett calls derivatives "financial weapons of mass destruction."

Although some of these instruments are finally headed toward central clearing, recordation, and standardized terms, they remain, by far, the biggest financial wild card in world history. Just like last time, should another crisis begin to materialize, nobody will know which institutions are on this derivatives hook.

And, boy, is it some giant hook: $800 trillion. That would be equal to—wait for it—eleven times *world* GDP. Some economists soothingly say, fear not: that's just the notional amount, and the actual amount at risk is maybe only something like $40 trillion (or merely three times the U.S. GDP). Whew! . . . Only 30x Lehman's net exposure when its collapse froze the world's financial systems last time around.

Moreover, the "too big to fail" banks, whose risks to the system were a primary target of the Dodd-Frank legislation, are now, you guessed it, even bigger. The top four banks now have 40% of the nation's deposits, so whatever that nice little piece of paper says, does anyone really think that the government will not bail one (or more) of them out in the face of a failure? Funny how making crises illegal doesn't seem to work out too often.

So, even as the world economies begin a collective sigh of relief that the previous crisis is subsiding, the next, and potentially bigger, one looms. The leverage machine is still enormous, critical, and subject to breakdown, just as in 2008.

Here's a little picture of how the commonalities of leverage, equity exposure, and, ironically, active risk management created a self-reinforcing loop that brought all the houses down together.

VALUE AT RISK / VICIOUS CIRCLE HYPOTHESIS

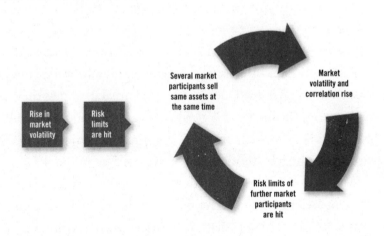

Source: Adapted and modified from Persaud (2000)

And here, by the way, is the answer to the big mystery of why gold initially fell during the big crisis in which it "should have" performed so well: it was one of the few assets that could be sold to raise cash for other needs. Great assets were dumped at fire sale prices, depressing other values in the process, requiring even more liquidations to meet more margin calls . . . and the spiral just continued from there. That's what a system-wide liquidity crisis will do for you.

Now, how about the stock market itself? Over there, the efficient, fair manifestation of Adam Smith's invisible hand, we have some serious shenanigans, too. More than two-thirds of exchange volume these days is high-frequency trading, about which you know: computers dueling with computers, trying to game the system and steal fractions of pennies out of the real trades that make up the rest of the activity. If that sounds dangerous and unstable, it is. But the exchanges prostrate themselves to encourage the trend because they make money from the volume of trading, not from the quality of the results for investors.

An ancillary development is the rise of "dark pools." These are places where stocks trade without the same kind of reporting that goes on with the public exchanges. That's what's "dark" about them. Initially they arose as places for very large institutional block trades to get done at the best price. But now, in many of the biggest stocks, more than half the volume is occurring in dark pools, and they are proliferating. Even the NYSE is getting in on the game. It says its model is only for retail investors and that the benefit to them will be sub-penny pricing, which has been a feature of dark pools for a while. Sounds awesome till you remember the size of a typical retail trade . . . on your next thousand-share sale, maybe you'll save $4. One doesn't have to be Sherlock Holmes to surmise that the real point is to ultimately win back the institutional volume it's been losing.

So there's a big trend toward more, different trading platforms with different rules, open to different sets of investors. You can spread total volume across only so many markets before it gets thin, and that hurts price transparency, liquidity, and stability.

Most fundamentally, if all the trading gets moved to platforms where people don't see the bid and ask, how does anyone know what the market for a particular stock really is?

Summarizing: record stockpiles of Buffett's "weapons of mass financial destruction" remain live ammo, while our banking sector is even more concentrated than last time and our stock markets are increasingly fragile. The resulting instability of our financial systems may not be the main reason to invest through alternative strategies, but it's not a bad one. After all, meltdowns are a lot more common than melt-ups, right? If you're long-only, it's hard to believe that you can be vigilant and fast enough to get out the next time the goblins get loose, as they surely will. Much better, in my view, to be invested through strategies that can absorb those losses, and through managers with the knowledge and access even to profit from the turmoil.

In Review

Beyond filling current job openings with specific investments lies the question of how to create the best panoramic, risk-tolerant portfolio from the giant menu of possible alternative investments. The suggestions in this chapter are a start.

Typical investors, those sitting on 60/40 portfolios today, should first exit bond funds to extinguish interest rate duration risk, and move into alternative income sources that rise with inflation. Step two is to reduce equity-driven volatility by migrating some long-only equity dollars into "smart beta" mutual funds and ETFs.

Illiquidity premiums are high these days, and investors who can afford to grab them probably should. In that context, the "liquidity ratio" is a helpful tool. Investors with LRs of 2 or 3 and higher should consider adding some less liquid alternatives; investors with LRs over 4 should almost certainly be in some privately placed hedge and venture vehicles, along with some real assets.

A truly risk-tolerant portfolio requires non-correlation and absolute diversification. Convergent and divergent strategies should be employed, and vulnerabilities must be checked across asset classes.

Before making long-term decisions, investors should consider the three big "regimes" that could dominate world economies over the next many years: inflation, deflation, and more "directionless volatility."

In the meantime, a careless match could easily ignite another financial conflagration. The dry tinder includes derivatives, excessive leverage, banking sector concentration, a hair-trigger stock market on technology steroids, and a world of geopolitical risks.

Final Thoughts

The most profound issues for long-term asset allocation concern the great inflation versus deflation fight; which wins out will have extraordinarily profound repercussions for investment strategies. But because the resulting outcomes could be so extreme, and so extremely different, it might be time to play chess, and make investment moves that serve more than one purpose. Among the few assets that meet this requirement are: control positions in cash-generating businesses; timber; TIPS; readily developable, well-located land; and gold.

CHAPTER 10

At the Dealership

A good rule of thumb is to assume that everything matters.
—RICHARD THALER

At this point you might well feel like doing at least a bit of window-shopping; maybe you're even interested in kicking the tires a bit on some of these new vehicles. Before heading over to the showroom, let's consider some general pointers and also some of the nitty-gritty issues you'll want to ask the dealer about.

The primary focus of this chapter is private transactions—investing in hedge, venture, and PE funds, and doing direct angel deals—because these are the most unfamiliar to most investors. But, of course, many of the issues regarding evaluation of hedge fund managers will also be pertinent to liquid alternatives and smart beta products; for example, when looking at mutual funds running hedged strategies, the **Sharpe** and **Sortino** ratios, described in the following section, will be important.

Hedge Funds

Once you've zoned in on a strategy and found a candidate fund, what should you look for? First, you want the manager to have substantial skin in the game—a big chunk of his personal liquid net worth invested—so that your interests are clearly aligned. Second, you want to see some sort of track record across different market cycles with good returns . . . and the statistics to show it wasn't luck.

Gross returns are naturally the headline and are usually reported as compound annual growth rate (**CAGR**, and pronounced "kayger"). This shows how dollars invested in the fund have grown over time. Big numbers are impressive, but there are several things to watch out for at the same time. One thing to examine is the fund's biggest historic **drawdown**, its largest loss, and how long it took to recover. You can also look at the percentage of months in which drawdowns occurred. Good start, but to really know what you're buying, it's important to understand a couple of key statistical measures as well.

Remember our ideally mediocre manager experiment from chapter 2? Even a fund that's been generating good returns might just have been lucky (so far). For a real-world example of how chasing returns, even while investing with famous guys, can turn out, take a look at Paulson & Co. A tsunami of subscriptions followed its flagship fund's 500% return in 2008, a feat of legend. And yet . . . it's suffered a precipitous decline since, down 50% in 2011 and another 25% or so in 2012. There's a lesson here.

What made Ted Williams the greatest hitter baseball's ever seen? According to him, it was not that he was just so amazingly skilled that he could hit anything thrown his way. He insisted, instead, the secret was all about "waiting for the fat pitch." The key was discipline, picking your spots. (And on the subject, here's a tip for your next trip to the greyhound track. The best way to win consistently is not to bet on every race, but to wait until one dog is so heavily favored that betting on the second and third favorites to win will return a nice profit if either of them does. In these pretty random races, that strategy, consistently applied, can pay for college, I can tell you.)

Maybe Ted Williams's dictum strikes you as obvious, but it requires a sort of patience that's hard while holding billions from people who are paying you fees to gamble their money. For Paulson, housing was indeed a very fat pitch; but subsequent big swings were taken at balls on the edge of the strike zone, or maybe even just outside it. The subprime mess was unique; and making similarly "bold" bets in cases without the same dynamics has generated exactly what the law of averages demands.

So you'd like to invest with fund managers who just swing at (and often hit) the fat pitches. But how can you tell? With two important statistical clues called the **Sharpe** and **Sortino** ratios. Other related measurements are described in the glossary,* but this pair is enough to get the idea, and even show off a bit at your next yacht club cocktail party.

The Sharpe ratio describes the return a manager generates *per unit of risk taken*. Now, that's one handy yardstick, but you may very fairly ask how "risk taken" is measured. Well, you may recall from chapter 4 that modern portfolio theory equates risk with volatility. So, essentially, the Sharpe ratio is equal to a manager's returns, divided by the volatility of those returns. Scores greater than 1 are good; better than 2, excellent; the number will appear in the fund's marketing materials.

Extremely useful, but a certain Mr. Sortino had a very excellent point about it: we don't hate all risk, just risk that doesn't work out so well. If a manager can really roll a seven every time, who's complaining? So he created a measurement that distinguishes "good volatility" from "bad volatility" and doesn't penalize a manager for

---

* **Information ratio**, R-squared, sigma, alpha, skew, and **kurtosis**.

taking risks that pay off. A fair analogy here is to a baseball player who hits lots of home runs, but doesn't strike out as much as most power hitters do . . . wait, we're back to Ted Williams. Hitting more homers than nearly anyone was upside deviation (as compared to the average player), but he didn't display the typical flip side, the downside deviation (as compared to average hitters) of many more Ks. As an investment manager, therefore, the Splendid Splinter would have had an awesome Sortino ratio, although a less stellar Sharpe.

So if you're comparing two managers who are generally trying to do the same thing, the Sharpe ratio can help identify who takes more risks, who takes less, and who does the better job at squeezing return from the risks he does assume. A little more sophisticated way of evaluating managers is the Sortino: you're really happy to meet a manager whose volatility is mostly upside, with fewer downside blips than average.

TIMING IS EVERYTHING

Roger Lowenstein's **When Genius Failed** tells the story of the most celebrated, and of course largest, hedge fund "implosion" in history, Long-Term Capital Management. Until Madoff, it was "the" reason to shy away from hedge funds. But the surprising story the book doesn't mention is that the average IRR for all investors from inception to final liquidation of LTCM—net of the "outrageous" 2 and 25 fee structure—was over 18%.

How could that be in a fund that imploded? Nearly everyone but the insiders had been mandatorily redeemed at the end of 1997, very close to the firm's all-time high-water mark. In a remarkable tale of the consequences of hubris, the managers wanted to keep all the results for themselves, and they succeeded.

The moral of the story—which on one level is banal, as it is told virtually monthly by Morningstar to mutual fund investors—is that "timing" is everything in hedge fund returns. Entry and exit points are more important, in most cases, than published returns as "dollars chase performance" and the actual experience of any given investor is often critically dependent on timing.

So, checking out a manager's gross returns, drawdowns, and Sharpe and Sortino ratios are the first steps in evaluating a fund. But that's just to determine whether it's worth a deeper look, because a totally different set of considerations is even more important: the operational side. More funds fail because of immature infrastructures than they do because of bad investments.

The org chart—especially risk management and compliance personnel—are vitally important. You'll also want to know about the internal processes: How are deals discovered and evaluated? Ask for some concrete examples of trades that went well, but also some that went badly. (How soon were they recognized, and what was done about them?) And one of the very best shorthand indicators that a fund is solid is its list of service providers: the accountants, lawyers, custodian, and compliance professionals (more on this below).

Now, the easy way to deal with these sorts of issues is to let someone else worry about it and default into extremely large, extremely well-established funds. That's fine, but it's also a good way to pay high fees for mediocre performance. Here's a little secret: most of the most amazing managers just won't take your money; they're closed to new investors. And many of the known names that will still take it have outgrown their alpha-generating days, but not their alpha-generating fee structures.

Study after study has shown that smaller funds substantially outperform bigger ones, and newer ones outperform older ones. Numerous reasons are suggested, but really these results are commonsensical. As we mentioned back in chapter 3, nearly all strategies are "capacity constrained" at some level; there's simply a limit on how big they can be and continue to work. Scale is the enemy of alpha: the inefficiencies still out there are small, with lots of smart posses in pursuit.

And then there's the very old-fashioned reason: scrappy young managers are simply trying extra hard in their first few years to produce the kinds of track records that will continue to attract larger investors. Right along with our core theme about alpha, many of these guys are just outworking the competition.

Nonetheless, those big funds are where all the big institutional money goes. Large institutions prefer to invest in bigger funds with subpar returns.

Yep, you read that right. As is true in every aspect of human endeavor, the bigger the institution, the more its decision makers are driven by risk aversion rather than by gain seeking. After all, the one thing that will get you fired is investing out of the mainstream, in an unknown fund that turns out to have some sort of operational problem down the road. No worries dropping big money by investing in name brands, but God forbid you should lose a dime in a no-name fund. Alas, as John Maynard Keynes said: "Worldly wisdom teaches us that it is better for reputation to fail conventionally than to succeed unconventionally."

Then there's the sheer size of the institutions themselves. If you've got to invest many billions, you can't bother to do the due diligence to write checks of less than, say, $100 million. And because you also don't want to be more than 10% of any given fund in which you're invested (again, too risky!), you can invest only in funds that already have $1 billion or more. The problem is further exacerbated by an industry of consultants and gatekeepers, who wrap many large allocators in a fabric impermeable to smaller funds regardless of their performance.

These factors converge to create the "AUM trap."*

Smaller managers may stamp out excellent track records, but when they go to big institutions for allocations, they get the treatment mentioned above. And when they go to smaller investors, like family offices, they get asked: Gee, if you're so great, why aren't you bigger?

That provides opportunities for the rest of us: the kinds of funds that demonstrate the best performance are the very ones open to new investors. Now, finding these smaller candidate funds can take some legwork . . . but not as much as before the Internet, or the advent of private placement advertising. The resource pages should help you.

Otherwise, several large money management institutions offer hedge fund "platforms" through which clients can invest in well-known shops. That is awfully convenient, but two caveats. First, the fees. The institution may well charge management and sales loads on top of the fund's 2 and 20 (or more, for a fund of funds). At a time when most investments are paying just a few percent a year, the total fees can look enormous. Second, the selection. These platforms often feature exactly the type of very large, very homogenized funds that have not performed terribly

---

* AUM = assets under management.

well over the past years. Many are just too big to deliver sustained alpha. And if you're only getting beta . . . why pay those fees?

Here are some other specific issues to consider when shopping for hedge funds. In addition to this checklist, you also might want to consider using one of the many high-quality, independent due diligence firms out there to vet the manager before investing. The relative cost is pretty modest, and the peace of mind it bestows is probably worth it.

- Rule number one: look for major "skin in the game" by the hedge fund manager.
- Ensure that the key members of the team have been together for a good while, and that the returns the fund is bragging about were generated with the current crew in charge.
- Unless you are working through expert consultants who are evaluating the fund and manager, limit yourself to advisors who are registered with the SEC. Not all have to be—the requirement typically applies only to firms with assets under management of $100 million and up—but why invest with an unregistered manager when so many good ones are subject to direct government oversight?
- Ensure that the service providers to the fund—the fund administrator, auditor, custody agent, prime broker, and legal counsel—are all "name brands." It is easy enough to make sure that everyone connected with the fund is a first-class organization with plenty to lose if things go wrong.

- Check fee structure details. For single manager funds, you know that "2 and 20" is the standard in the industry. Sometimes you can do a bit better, but that's still the going rate for top managers. "Funds of funds" are usually more like 1 and 10, or sometimes 0 and 15 (we like "zero"!). But also watch for two very important provisions regarding how exactly these fees are calculated.

First, a **hurdle rate**. The idea here is that the 20% profits interest doesn't kick in until the fund returns surpass a specified annual level, which only seems fair: why pay 20% fees on money you could have earned in a standard investment. Second, a **high-water mark** provision, which ensures that the manager gets his incentive profits interest only as the fund hits new *all-time* highs, and not as the manager merely rebounds after a big drop-off.

- **Lockups**. It used to be that two-year lockups were common, but one year is now the rule, with quarterly redemptions thereafter. Some funds require no lockups at all, which sounds great but may not be as big a bonus as it appears.

Some strategies simply take time to develop and work—distressed credit strategies are a good example. In those cases, you don't want co-investors who are "hot money," dollars that will fly away at the wrong moment and wreck a trading strategy. So, as attractive as it sounds, "no lockup" can have its own costs.

- **Gates**. The importance of understanding "gates" has been underscored by the travails of the large and well-known Endowment Fund, which recently informed investors that it would limit their abilities to withdraw funds even though their lockups had expired. The fund held both liquid and illiquid investments, and early redemptions required disposal of a disproportionate percentage of the former. Faced with holding far too large a weighting in longer term investments, it brought down its gates and limited further withdrawals. The money is now both locked away and subjected to ongoing heavy fees. Ouch.

Note also that gates create a real "game theory" problem. If everyone knows that only the first, say, 25% of requesters can get out without waiting, a powerful dynamic is created to rush for the door at any hint of trouble . . . which actually exacerbates the liquidity crunch the fund is attempting to prevent. Although "gates" may be unavoidable in some strategies, not all funds need gates or should have them. A true long/short equity fund, for example, should be able to liquidate its positions on short notice without undue harm to the book, or to the investors who remain.

PE and Venture Capital Funds

As far as the selection process goes, PE and VC funds share most characteristics, so we'll treat the two together. And right off the top here's the headline: investing with the very top managers has been extremely profitable for many years. Investing with second-tier guys, not so much. Here's the PE chart, but the VC chart doesn't look much different.

SELECTING THE RIGHT PE FUND MANAGER IS VITAL

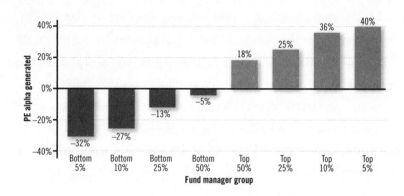

Analysis includes only fund managers with at least ten realized transactions; analysis based in gross deal returns, not net fees to LPs.

Source: "Private Equity Study: Finding Alpha 2.0," Oliver Gottschalg, HEC-Paris; Golding Capital Partners, November 2011

Thus, focus on track record is exceptionally important. Well-performing PE and venture managers tend to keep doing well; underperformers tend to keep lagging. Indeed, here's a great heuristic: pick funds with high serial numbers. A given firm's "Fund 3" or, even better, "Fund 7" probably indicates previous success. Like software, it's risky to try version 1.0.

Note how different this is from hedge funds, where many of the best opportunities are with newer, smaller outfits. Why would that be? Number one: PE and VC funds require great sources of deal flow . . . something that's generated by previous success. Hedge fund managers, in contrast, are buying and selling public securities that require no special access. In addition, PE and VC firms compete on the basis of large pools of available capital, human resources, and relationship networks; none are required of hedge funds, and none are strengths of first-time PE and VC funds.

Here's the most basic question you can ask at the PE/VC showroom: have the previous funds actually returned a nice multiple of their investors' money . . . say, 2x to 4x? And if there has been only one great return, was it due to a non-repeatable event?

You'll also want to ask the same questions about the firm's infrastructure as you would about a hedge fund's. But the really big question to ask about a PE fund is what kind of **waterfall** it has: European or American. That's not because we're going sightseeing.

Playing in the Waterfall

We've mentioned many times that "2 and 20" is a standard for these funds. But there's an exceptionally large devil in the details here.

Let's say we've invested in a real estate PE fund that's made six different investments of its own. The happy day arrives in which the first one is sold, and the fund makes a good profit on it. Time for a distribution! Let's also say the investors have put $100 million total into the fund, and that it bought this particular property for $10 million and sold it for $20 million. Who gets what?

In the European-style waterfall, the answer is easy: all the money goes back to the investors, because they've invested much more than $20 million into the fund. The manager's fee split doesn't kick in until the investors have been paid back their total fund investment, plus a preferred return of perhaps 6% or 8%.

The American-style waterfall is much more manager-friendly: he gets paid on a deal-by-deal basis, instead of waiting until all the investors' dollars have been returned. So in this example the

first $10 million of proceeds would go back to the investors, be-
cause that's the amount of investment this particular deal took.
Then, they'd also get paid their preferred return on that $10 mil-
lion (say, $600,000). But then, in the U.S. pattern, the manager
will collect his roughly $2 million of profits from the remaining
$9.4 million. He doesn't have to wait for several more deals to be
liquidated so the limited partners can get full recovery of their
total original investments.*

Angel Investing

Beyond the discussion in chapter 7 and the suggestions to join
an angel group and use the available online resources, we won't
try to describe the decision process regarding which start-ups
to support . . . that's a whole other book. Just remember that no
matter how much you love the idea, ensure the entrepreneur has
skin in the game. As with a hedge fund manager, you want total
alignment and sense of urgency.

But we will address one very fundamental conundrum, which
is: Once you've decided that you do want to invest, how, exactly,
should you do it?

There are two big schools of thought here. One is that you
should go ahead and buy stock of the start-up, just like the institutions do. The second is that you should "punt" on all the tough
issues involved in a stock purchase and just fund through a much
simpler "next round note."

Let's start with the harder road. Generally, venture firms in-

---

* If you're seriously evaluating one of these, check out **clawback** and **catch-up** in
the glossary.

vest in start-ups through convertible preferred stock. The convertible preferred converts into common 1:1, so you're effectively buying common stock of the start-up, but with lots of protections in it regarding your stock rights, dilution, things like that. That's fine, but the really important question is, upon conversion, what percentage of the company will you get, assuming no further investment? In other words, what the heck is the thing worth?

That usually requires a tough negotiation, for entrepreneurs are inherently wildly optimistic. You, of course, want the valuation of the company to be as low as possible to maximize your percentage. Good luck. But remember, if you do have that discussion, make sure you're on the same page from day one about whether the number you're talking about is **pre-** or **post-money**; otherwise there will be some real consternation when that misunderstanding becomes apparent.

Once that's decided, the rest of the documentation process becomes very much easier. Over the past few years, a few sets of reasonably standard documents have come into use that avoid all the (often silly) negotiations that eat up lawyer time and critical dollars. For years, that had been a huge problem in start-up land: if a seed round is only for, say, $300k, you don't want to spend $50k on legal fees—or burn the time to negotiate documents, especially because a lot of entrepreneurs were pretty unsophisticated about what should be in them.

One popular set of these standard documents is called "Series Seed." The name is a riff on the usual industry lingo, in which the first institutional round has been called "Series A," moving deeper into the alphabet as the company matures and raises capital at (with luck) higher valuations. Series Seed documents are available for free online. This particular effort is from Marc Andreessen (of Netscape and Andreessen Horowitz fame), and the docs were drafted by an excellent law firm. There are a few other sets out there, too, from Y Combinator, the NVCA, Gust.com, and one or two others. They are all fairly similar, "Series A Light" convertible preferred documents.

So that's way number one. The alternative, quite popular with individuals, is a "next round note." The big advantage is that this kicks the can down the road on that often contentious valuation discussion. Here, the investment takes the form of a convertible loan instead of a convertible stock.

How? The big trick is that the invested amount is initially documented as a loan, but the loan converts into equity in the next investment round, when the value of the company will be set. Kicking the can down the road in this way isn't cheating at all, for that next round will usually involve professional angels or VCs who have more experience with such things, and also occur after more is known about the company's prospects.

To compensate for the fact that the earlier investors took more risk, the conversion will be at a discount to that next round's valuation. So, if the initial group of investors puts up $200,000 in a next round note, and later on VCs come in to the company with a pre-money valuation of $4 million, the initial group might wind up with 10% of the company instead of the 5% they'd get on that straight math.

The convertible note route also lets everyone avoid other issues that typically are negotiated in a stock deal, like antidilution ratchets.

For ease and speed, next round notes are unbeatable. Professional investors don't like to use them, however, because they can create something of a misalignment of interests. When the notes do convert in that subsequent round, the entrepreneur will want that valuation to be as high as possible, and so would an early investor who held stock. But a convertible note holder will want to see a lower company valuation because then his loan will convert into a higher equity percentage. It's a fair point, but probably not a big enough deal to worry about in noninstitutional rounds.

Picking CTAs

At the moment, 10% of the biggest CTAs control 90% of industry assets, up from 80% ten years ago. And knowing what we do about scale being the enemy of alpha, it's quite predictable that these managers will revert to the mean and deliver more correlation than investors would like. In some ways that might not matter, for like tippity-top VC and PE firms, top CTAs almost pick you: their minimums are at least hundreds of thousands, and often meaningfully more.

So you're likely looking at an emerging manager as your first entry into the game. In that hunt, the (audited) track record's the thing. Because you will open a heavily regulated, separately managed account rather than invest through a commingled vehicle, there's less pressure on the various infrastructure diligence issues that accompany hedge, PE, and VC fund investments. The SMA structure offers transparency and rapid liquidity, and the advisor is overseen by the National Futures Association and the Commodities Futures Trading Commission.

The very first stop for new investors should be the National Futures Association Web site. It's loaded with information and provides important background information on all properly registered CTAs.

In analyzing that track record, our friends Sharpe and Sortino are once again very useful in evaluating the manager's risk-adjusted returns. But with CTAs, another measure is also helpful, and that's called the "MTE": the margin-to-equity ratio. This provides a good shorthand way to check how volatile (risky) a CTA's positions are. It indicates how much of his account can be used for margin purposes—the futures exchanges set those limits in accordance with the riskiness of the trader's positions. A rule of thumb is that MTE ratios in excess of 10% might show you a CTA who's too adventurous for a starting investor.

Red and Yellow Flags

High YTB Products

The avalanche of new alternative investment products includes several with an extraordinarily high "YTB." This is definitely not to be confused with "YTM," the standard "yield to maturity," which measures the return on a bond until redemption. A high YTM is great, but a high YTB is very bad: it stands for "yield to broker."

The usual suspects for high YTB products include IPOs of closed-end, income-oriented funds, especially those holding MLPs and BDCs. If you like the products, stay away from the initial offering, and buy in the aftermarket. A host of "structured products" are similar. These are often issued by large financial institutions, and promise returns tied to some index, often with both a floor and a leveraged return for the upside. A typical one might be a $1,000 interest-bearing note tied to the Nikkei: it will return your capital if that market is down, but pay out an additional $1 for every $2 that the index is up over 10%. There are countless permutations of these sorts of formulas in a wide variety of instruments, usually driven by the issuer's ability to buy big swaps and derivatives contracts at, effectively, wholesale prices, and then break them down for sale to smaller investors at retail. That doesn't mean that they're always bad deals, but do be extremely careful to check all the charges and fees.

Nonlisted BDCs and REITs

A fairly substantial industry has evolved around "nontraded REITs." The sales pitch, articulated with an entirely straight face, claims that the fact they are *not* listed on an exchange is actually a big bonus, you see, because investors aren't exposed to the ups and downs of the market. That's a little like saying you should buy a car without an engine because, after all, it'll never be in a wreck. Please be extra cautious with these. They tend to be very high YTB products, have a poor investment track record as a class, and of course lack one of the most critical benefits of most REITS: liquidity. Precisely the same concerns apply to non-traded business development companies.

Leveraged ETFs

You might think that, strategy aside, all ETFs are pretty much the same, but that's not the case. First, you should always ensure that the sponsor of the ETF is a large, well-known institution, and that the ETF itself has substantial assets under management ($1 billion or more). Otherwise, you could wind up in an ETF that simply fails; you should get your money back, but that's not why you're investing.

There's also an important new development, the "actively managed" ETF, which essentially turns the basic idea (passively indexed investing) on its head, and delivers something more like mutual fund management in an ETF wrapper. All well and good, but watch the fees—you don't necessarily get the typical ETF operating expense advantage that you'd expect.

The one ETF to totally avoid is the "leveraged ETF." These promise things like double, or even triple, returns on a move in some index. But because of a mathematical trick, you're nearly always unpleasantly surprised by the results if you hold the securities for any length of time. Just imagine an ETF that promises to pay 2x the move of the S&P. You're bullish, and buy it at $100. Next day, the market goes up 10%; and the following day, it goes down 10%. Even so far, right?

Wrong. On day one, it does go to $120 (it adds 2 times 10% of 100), and you're happy; but on day two, it goes down to $96 (it loses 2 times 10% of 120). So it hasn't moved, but you're behind. This sort of "tracking error" compounds very rapidly, often leaving investors mystified about why they've been right on the overall direction of an index over a period, but way behind where they expected to be as a result.

In Review

Doing the work to decide whether to invest in a private transaction can seem a bit overwhelming, but an awful lot of it is just common sense: Is the management team of unquestioned integrity? Do the professional advisors have the right pedigrees? Do the principals' economic incentives align with those of the investors? What's the track record look like?

Whether investing in hedge funds or in angel deals, make sure the investment manager or entrepreneur has skin in the game; is hungry; and is dedicated to having a robust, full-fledged business organization around that fabulous strategy.

For liquid strategies, pay attention to the classic metrics that help tell the lucky from the good. If you have to pick one, go with Sortino. Also check to make sure the fund's largest "drawdown" was within your tolerance, and find out how long it took to recover.

Pay very close attention to the details of the fee structures of hedge funds and PE funds. Hurdles, high-water marks, lockups, and gates are important.

In PE funds, European-style waterfalls are infinitely preferable to American-style.

On the angel investing front, "next round notes" are the easiest way to handle pre-institutional investment rounds. If you go to more traditional stock issuances, stick closely to available free and online documentation.

When evaluating a CTA, check him out on the NFA site, examine his audited track record, and look for a low MTE ratio.

And avoid high "YTB" products; leveraged ETFs; and nontraded BDCs and REITs.

Final Thought

Making investments in nontraded instruments may seem a little daunting, and, at least the first few times you enter unfamiliar territory, you might well want to work with trusted advisors who've been there before. But even if you do, it's good to understand the basics laid out in this chapter. You'll become a better, smarter investor quickly.

Conclusion: It's Time!

Just as I was turning in the final draft of this book, the National Intelligence Council issued its "Global Trends 2030" report. It reflects the joint assessment of the sixteen U.S. intelligence agencies about the world's likely fate over the next many years.

Their central thesis may sound familiar: the uncertainty level has never been higher, and extraordinarily different kinds of worlds might emerge from the current cauldron of new global forces. The study lists several "megatreands" of particular concern, including: the end of U.S. global dominance; the powerfully disruptive force of technology development; increasing water, food, and energy scarcities; and increasing political instability. The intelligence agencies then assembled a list of their likely possible "game changers," risks that could fundamentally alter the future for all of us.

The number one concern? A collapse of the "crisis-prone global economy." You can therefore ignore all of my fretting throughout the book and listen to theirs instead . . . they are, after all, much better qualified worriers than I am. And maybe there's even a clue in the title of the report: "Alternative Worlds."

It is time—right now—to adopt a fundamentally different mind-set about your investments. The periodic crashes that have bedeviled 60/40 portfolios in the past are nearly certain to repeat. Alternative investing strategies do in fact give nearly every investor the ability to improve his chances of surviving the next one(s) in decent shape; but they won't help if you don't use them. And please don't think the markets will send you a gentle reminder memo just before the next crisis.

Simultaneously, the report inherently points to enormous potential investing upsides in new technologies, in the goods and services that will be demanded by mushrooming middle classes around the globe, and in infrastructure to support all that growth. Massive new wealth creation will indeed occur, but only a small sliver of it will be captured in traditional U.S. stocks.

Don't worry, after all these pages of hammering I'm not going to repeat all the ideas of the book here. But I am going to underline once more that *our old investing perspectives will not work going forward*. The world is changing, whether we like it or not, at a scary pace. Risks have multiplied hugely, while the opportunity sets have changed drastically.

Of course I don't know your personal financial circumstances, but here's my guess: you cannot afford to ignore those facts.

Acknowledgments

Hollis Heimbouch is the publisher you pray for: someone with the vision to identify a coming trend, and the courage to commit to it before everyone else catches on and makes it comfortable. But that's just the start, for her intelligence, humor, and powerful encouragement contributed very directly to the end result. The book world is lucky to have found her before the venture capital world did, and I'm incredibly grateful that she deemed this little start-up worthy of her energies.

It was exhilarating to work with her.

Indeed, you can be envious of the super team she's assembled at HarperCollins, since they have that pleasure every day. But Katie O'Callaghan's refrain after our first meeting, "I'm all about timber," signaled that it's no one-way street; Hollis is pretty lucky, too. Colleen Lawrie's patience and diligence and Joanna Pinsker's enthusiasm were very much appreciated.

But I only met Hollis & Co. through the auspices of my wonderful agent and dear friend Susan Ginsburg, who has risked her sterling reputation more than once on my behalf. Indeed, I owe her for much more than that: it was she who got me writing in the first place. You may consider that good or ill; but it's on her. So, Susan, thank you very much for everything you've done for me.

Now, very obviously, a book like this could not possibly cover so many topics well without the invaluable assistance of numerous experts.

Tom Mahoney served as my overall genius resource and also did one heck of a job editing early drafts; and my longtime friend

Lee O'Dwyer also did yeoman's duty to tune up the work and help clarify key ideas. Beyond them, as you can imagine, is a long list of sector specialists who were overly generous with their time: Jim Rickards (gold, hedge funds, overlay); Sean O'Shea (real estate); Brian O'Donoghue (distressed and activist investing); Jim Jubak (global blue chips); David S. Rose (angel investing); Howard Morgan (venture capital); Brad Alford (hedged equity strategies); Neil Berger (funds of funds); Sarah Zaros (emerging markets); Jon Sundt and Andrea Trachenburg (managed futures funds); Mark Melin (CTAs); Sandy Kemper (art); Tony Davidow (ETFs); Randy Kenworthy (oil and gas); Scott Rickards (water); and Guy Haselmann (fixed income). Arnie and Sandy Peinado, along with Bill and Mariella Greene, provided key insights about power generation in the aftermath of Hurricane Sandy. And very many thanks also to hardworking reviewers and researchers Ritu Khanna, Noah Levin, Suraj Patel, and Adam Scott.

Deirdre Bolton, Bloomberg's phenomenal television journalist, is really a coauthor of many of the thoughts expressed in this book. I am thankful to her not only for that, but also for having the vision to launch the first daily programming dedicated to alternative investing—and including my "Buzzword" segments. It's a funny thing about TV anchors: they're very well known, but only for a limited set of their skills. So you might not appreciate, as I have come to understand, just how seriously smart, insightful, and hardworking she is. A pro's pro, who, I'm happy to report, has become a trusted friend.

But even more special thanks have to go out to two others. One is my fantastic editor, to whom I'm also very fortunately married, Lenore; and the other is my father-in-law, Joe, the first to read and comment on every draft (and there were lots!).

Glossary

13D: A form filed with the SEC when an activist investor goes over 5% ownership of a traded company. It's a public document, and 13D filings are watched closely by many investors; some mutual funds even invest only in companies for which 13Ds have been filed. Item 4 is the key provision; that's where the investor states his intention, which might include launching a proxy fight, initiating a takeover, or forcing change in management. A nonactivist investor who exceeds 5% ownership files a 13G instead.

ABSOLUTE DIVERSIFICATION: A principle of portfolio construction that minimizes the number of investments vulnerable to a given economic risk or regime, recognizing that many superficially different strategies can be felled by a single type of event. Key risks to consider in this regard: credit freezes, duration, counterparty concentration, geographic, geopolitical, illiquidity.

ABSOLUTE RETURN: Literally and simply, the total gain or loss on a portfolio; but the term connotes hedge fund strategy returns. It is meant to emphasize the difference with traditional managers, who are measured by their performance *relative* to a benchmark, like the S&P.

ACCREDITED INVESTOR: An individual with a net worth of at least $1 million, not including his residence, or who meets certain annual income tests; the definition also includes most institutions. With limited exceptions, investors not meeting this test generally may not purchase private placements. Note that a fund manager may not charge incentive management fees except to investors who are also "qualified clients" (see below).

ALGO TRADING: Trading that uses sophisticated computer programs to make automated decisions, with no humans involved in individual transactions. Very common in managed futures investing and a bedrock of high-frequency trading and "quants."

ALPHA: In the common parlance of modern portfolio theory, this is the extra return that a liquid security asset manager generates over a benchmark against which he's measured (like the S&P), but only to the extent he didn't take additional risk to do it. See also "Sharpe ratio" and "Sortino ratio."

In the more general sense of this book, alpha is the value added by an active manager in any asset class or strategy through skill and hard work. For example, venture capitalists and TIMOs can and do provide "alpha" even though they're operating in illiquid markets and where the term does not technically apply.

BACKWARDATION: In the futures market, backwardation is a pricing phenomenon in which near-month contracts are more expensive than those for later delivery. It's the opposite of the more common contango.

BETA: Beta is a measure of the correlation that the performance of a stock or portfolio has to the overall movement of the markets, but is not exactly the same idea. For example, if a stock is always up 20% when the market is up 10%, there is a correlation of 1, because they always move together. But the beta is 2, because the stock is up twice as much as the index. Generally, lower-beta stocks offer less risk than the overall market, and the higher-beta stocks offer more.

BETA NEUTRAL: One key test for whether a "market neutral" fund really is: do the long and short sides have offsetting betas?

BLACK-SCHOLES: This is the formula that solved an ancient puzzle about how to value an option. The key insight was to reference the historic volatility of the underlying security: the more
volatile the performance has been, the more valuable an option
to buy or sell it is, at least from an academic point of view. See
"implied volatility."

BLACK SWAN FUNDS: These are meant to do well when the markets go haywire, and invest in options and derivates that pay
off when very extreme movements and events occur. (See
pages 122–26.)

BUSINESS DEVELOPMENT CORPORATION, "BDC": BDCs are special investment vehicles for direct investment in middle market
and smaller companies. Some do debt deals, some do equity,
some do both. They have to pay out essentially all income to
shareholders and do not pay tax at the entity level, a bit like a
REIT or MLP. (See pages 92–93.)

CAGR, COMPOUND ANNUAL GROWTH RATE (PRONOUNCED "KAY-
GER"): A common way to measure returns for investments in
funds and liquid securities. You take the bookends: how much
was invested on day one, how much came back on day x,
and then figure out what compounded annual rate explains the
difference. CAGR is comparable to an IRR return calculation.

CALMAR RATIO: A performance measure of investment managers
that divides a manager's CAGR over the most recent three-
year period by the largest drawdown during that time. Therefore, the higher, the better.

CARRY TRADE: See "funding currency" (and page 132).

CAT BONDS: These are high-yield bonds issued by insurance companies as a way to lay off the risks of a big catastrophe, most
commonly hurricanes. The good news is that investors don't
face the same credit risk as they do with typical high-yield

issues; but the bad news is that, if a specified disaster strikes, the payments either are reduced or stop altogether. (See pages 85–87.)

CATCH-UP: In many PE and real estate deals, investors are paid a preferred return before the manager's incentive compensation kicks in. The question is, after that, exactly how does the manager "catch up" regarding profits paid out to the investors— how exactly are the next dollars shared?

CLAWBACK: Contractual provisions requiring a manager to give back compensation previously received when performance falls below a specified level; most commonly seen in "American-style" PE waterfalls where the first one or two exits are successful, but subsequent ones aren't.

CLOSED-END FUNDS (CEFS): The counterpart to a traditional, open-end mutual fund. These do not issue shares directly to, or redeem them directly from, investors; instead, the number of shares is fixed, and they trade on an exchange like a stock. As a result, they can hold less liquid instruments and are sometimes used to house longer-term alternative strategies. (See pages 61–62.)

CONTANGO: This describes a pricing condition in which futures contracts for a commodity are more expensive for months further into the future than they are for months closer to the present time (the opposite of backwardation). This can present issues in some commodity ETFs, which automatically sell out of nearer term contracts (to avoid delivery requirements) and buy longer-dated ones; the fund may experience a loss even though the spot price of the commodity hasn't changed.

CONVERGENT STRATEGIES: Strategies that assume the prices of securities will "converge" over time to some inherent value or relationship. Most "relative value" and "pairs" trades qualify, as do most kinds of arbitrage. These strategies work best in normal market environments when classic modern portfolio theory is operating, but they tend to do badly amid serious market disruptions, and when the forces of behavioral economics take hold. (See pages 72–73.)

CONVERTIBLE ARBITRAGE: A strategy that focuses on the implied price of the conversion option embedded in convertible bond versus the price for a separate, traded option. (See pages 106–8.)

CONVEXITY: The price of a bond usually falls less for a given increase in rates than it rises for an equally large fall in rates. When you chart that out, you get a convex curve, hence the name. And, *all other things being equal*, bonds with high convexity are more desirable than bonds with lower convexity. They display more of that happy characteristic that the upside is greater than the downside for a given move in interest rates.

CREDIT DEFAULT SWAP: These arose as types of insurance policies for credit instruments, actually structured as swaps: in the event of default, the insuring party will receive the actual cash flows on the bond, and the insured party will get a specified set of payment equal to the interest and principal the bond would have paid absent the default.

CTA: Commodities trading advisors are the managers behind "managed futures," below. They typically trade algorithmic strategies keyed off trends in commodity prices. Generally, all investors in a given strategy will have the same investments and results—CTAs do not customize portfolios for individuals as RIAs do. Always check a CTA's background on the National Futures Association Web site, and the audited track record of a strategy, before investing.

DELTA: Delta refers to the relationship between the price of an option or other derivative to buy or sell an asset and the asset itself (known as the "underlying"). Those prices do not usually move in complete lockstep.

DELTA NEUTRAL: A portfolio or position adjusted over time to account for changes in delta.

DENOMINATOR EFFECT: Most institutional investors have target allocations for asset classes. In the crash of 2007–8, the "whole pie" shrank (the denominator got smaller) and illiquid positions that couldn't be sold suddenly became too large a percentage of the total. Rebalancing has required avoidance of more illiquids (and/or distressed selling of existing positions).

DISCOUNT RATE: Here we don't meant the Fed's "discount rate" but instead the assumed rate at which a pension plan will generate growth to pay for future obligations. The higher the rate, the less the need for current contributions (and the less underfunded the plan looks); the lower the rate, the higher the need for current contributions (and the more underfunded it looks). Most states actually require an 8% discount rate to be used, even though that's wildly optimistic in the current environment; the Government Accounting Standards Board is trying to implement rules that would force states to use more realistic assumptions.

DISTRESSED INVESTING: An investment strategy in which the manager selects securities that he believes are fundamentally underpriced, and works to have their true value recognized. The majority of distressed investors focus on bonds and bank loans of troubled companies, and taking companies into and through the bankruptcy process is often a key part of the strategy. (See pages 135–36.)

DIVERGENT STRATEGIES: As you'd guess, the opposite of "convergent" ones. Divergent strategies key off of basic supply-and-demand questions rather than historical price relationships

and patterns. Global macro, managed futures, currency trading, and numerous niche strategies can all qualify and tend
to do comparatively well amid market disruption. (See pages
72–73.)

DOLLAR NEUTRAL: A method of measuring a long/short portfolio's neutrality: are the dollars on both sides of the book equal,
meaning no net investment?

DRAWDOWN: This is the maximum percentage loss that the manager or fund has experienced; usually, it is measured "peak to
valley"—the highest absolute point to the lowest, which can
happen over an extended period. By the way, it isn't related to
withdrawals from a fund, the percentage of money that's been
pulled out by investors . . . that's a common confusion.

DRY POWDER: Capital ready for investment by PE, venture, and
angel investors. PE firms take in big capital commitments up
front, before they start making investments; those accumulated but unspent dollars are the firm's dry powder. VC and
angel investors must keep dry powder around for follow-on
investments; the start-up will require more money later, and
early investors can be badly diluted if they are not in a position
to participate in subsequent rounds.

DURATION RISK: You know that as interest rates rise, bond prices
fall. But not all bonds suffer by the same amount, percentage
wise. Other factors being equal, bonds with longer maturities
will fall relatively more than shorter duration bonds. Bonds
with lower coupon bonds will fall relatively more than higher
coupon bonds. Both of those facts stem from the bond's duration, which is the measure of the time it takes for an investor to
recover his investment in it. The longer the duration of a bond,
the more sensitive its price is to rising interest rates.

EBITDA: Earnings before interest, taxes, depreciation, and amortization: that is, how much money is being made in the running of the business? Often shortened to EBIT, it's an extremely common metric for establishing private company valuations and purchase prices.

EFFICIENT MARKET HYPOTHESIS: An underlying principle of modern portfolio theory that holds that markets constantly re-adjust securities prices for all information through the bidding of rational investors.

ENDOWMENT MODEL: Also known as "strategic asset allocation," a theory of portfolio composition that emphasizes extremely broad portfolios, including substantial allocations to less liquid investments such as private equity and venture capital. David Swenson of Yale is the acknowledged pioneer, and numerous other large endowments subsequently adopted the approach.

ETFs: Exchange-traded funds (see pages 59–60) hold a basket of securities, usually one that mirrors a given index, like the S&P. Buying a share of the fund gives an investor a fractional interest in the basket. Fund shares trade on ex-changes, just like stocks. They tend to have lower operat-ing expenses than mutual funds because (1) most are not actively managed; and (2) they do not require the internal plumbing to constantly issue and redeem shares. On the other hand, trading involves brokerage fees not present with no-load mutual funds.

Now, if you think about it for a second, you'll come to this question. Is that a free ride for the ETF? If it has a fixed set of securities inside it, and it doesn't redeem out and issue new shares like a mutual fund, how do you keep the price of the fund from getting out of whack with the total prices of the underlying securities? In traded closed-end funds (CEFs), for example, we know that the market price is usually different from the total prices of the securities in the fund. But that would blow the whole reason for investing in ETFs.

The big trick is something called an "authorized participant" or "AP." These are specified financial institutions outside the fund. Say that the AP sees that the price of the ETF is getting too high in relation to the stocks inside it . . . there's more demand for the ETF shares than there is supply. The AP goes into the market and buys a basket of stocks that exactly replicates the holdings of the ETF. It then delivers that basket of stocks to the fund, in exchange for new ETF shares. And it then sells those shares into the market, which brings the price of the ETF back into line. The AP makes a small profit on the arbitrage there. That's why the ETF prices stay in line with their underlying investments: APs are constantly out there arbitraging away any price disparities, by forcing either the issuance or the redemption of ETF shares.

So, in a nutshell, with ETFs, the APs and the market are performing that function, whereas mutual funds have to do it themselves. All else being equal, ETFs are cheaper to operate. But, as we mentioned before, they're usually more expensive to buy and sell.

ETNs: Exchange-traded notes, like ETFs, are indeed traded on an exchange. Both are ways of investing in indexes tied to specific asset classes. But the structures are very different in crucial ways, as the *f* to *n* switch implies. These are notes, debt obligations of the issuer, often a large bank like Barclays or Morgan. But unlike a typical loan, the amount of principal and interest you get back is tied to the performance of a given asset class index. The biggest downside is that, with an ETN, you're an unsecured creditor of a single institution.

F&F: The "friends and family" round is the first outside capital into a start-up and predates the first professional money from angel investors or VCs.

FIRST MOVER/FAST FOLLOWER: A first mover invents something new and has the advantage of being first to market; the idea is to grab early users, get feedback, and iterate more quickly than later entrants can. But first movers can also make a lot of instructive mistakes. Smart observers of the scene can learn from those mistakes and become successful "fast followers."

FREEMIUM: The dominant business model in the digital world. The idea is to give away your core product or service, drive massive usage of it, and then offer a premium service that some percentage (usually a very small one) of the users will choose to buy. LinkedIn and Dropbox are good examples.

FUNDING CURRENCY: In a carry trade, an investor borrows in the currency of a low-interest-rate jurisdiction (say Japan), and uses the proceeds to invest in a country with a higher interest rate (say Australia). The borrowed currency is called the funding currency. (See pages 132–33.)

Borrowing at 1% and lending at, say, 3% is a pretty good trade, provided that the relative strengths of the currencies involved don't change. In the example, at some point the yen loan has to be repaid. The risk is that the yen appreciates while the loan is out, making repayment more expensive.

GAMMA: Refers to the change in delta (see above) over time . . . that is, how much a derivative's *sensitivity* to price of the security underlying the derivative fluctuates.

GATES: These are mechanisms that keep investors from pulling the money out of hedge and private equity funds even after an investor's lockup has ended. Aside from the fact that managers want to keep as much money in the fund as possible, the rationale is that if too much money leaves at once, the manager may have to break trades at unfavorable moments.

GIPS: Stands for Global Investment Performance Standard, published by the CFA Institute, for hedge fund managers. GIPS requires a *time-weighted* methodology, not *a dollar-weighted* methodology. In general, time-weighted methodologies are the industry standard for hedge funds because they trade liquid securities; dollar-weighted performance, like IRR, is preferred for private equity.

GLOBAL MACRO FUNDS: Global macro managers are top-down, big-picture traders. They generally don't engage in the same sort of relative value and arbitrage-type strategies that most hedge funds do. Global macro is a "divergent" strategy that tends to do well when more traditional strategies do poorly. (See pages 130–33.)

GREEKS: "The Greeks" refers to five measures of the way the price of a derivative relates to the price of the "underlying"— the asset to which the derivative relates. Aside from the well-known delta and gamma (see above), they include theta, for time sensitivity; and rho for interest rate sensitivity. Vega is sensitivity to volatility, but it is a bit of a cheat: there's no V in the Greek alphabet.

GREENSHOE: This is a provision that allows a company to issue up to 15% more stock in the IPO process than they originally said they would. Normally, people think of it as something that allows a company in a very successful IPO to issue more shares and take advantage of the popularity of the offering, but it can also work to support the price when the shares come under pressure, as happened in the Facebook IPO.

Knowing that a greenshoe can be invoked, underwriters effectively short a stock by overallocating it in the IPO. If it goes up, they can cover the short with the greenshoe, with the net impact of just having sold more stock. But if it falls, they cover the short from the market, thus adding buying support.

HEDGE FUND: A private partnership that invests in liquid securities and actively manages risks through shorting or other offsetting positions (hedging!). They may or may not deploy leverage to increase returns. Most hedge funds pursue "relative value" approaches such as equity or credit long/short strategies; others engage in distressed, activist, and global macro styles. Generally, managers are paid 2% of the assets under management as a base fee plus 20% of the profits. (See pages 207–16.)

HFT: "High-frequency trading" refers to systems that use superior connection speeds and superfast algorithms to exploit slower stock exchange participants (in ways explained in the text). Advantages of a few billionths of a second are adequate to convey meaningful trading opportunities, and well more than half the volume on the exchanges is generated by HFT. It is widely believed that these systems add meaningfully to stock market instability. (See pages 119–20.)

HIGH-WATER MARK: This is an important provision for investors to have in any compensation arrangement under which a manager takes a share of a fund's profits. The idea is that, say, the typical 20% is taken only as the fund's total returns keep hitting new highs; no fair to claim it after being down 50% in one year, then back up 30% the next.

HORIZON ARBITRAGE: Many investors are coming around to the idea that there's simply too much focus on the short term in investing and longer term values are being ignored. Strategies that aim at that disparity are sometimes called (time) "horizon arbitrage" plays. The term is probably used the most to describe activist and distressed investors, who expect to work for a long time before they get the result they are looking for. It's a reminder of one theme of the book: alpha takes work, and work takes time.

HURDLE RATE: Like "high-water mark," this is an important investor protection in funds that pay percentages of profits to their managers. The hurdle rate (also called a preference) is the amount an investor earns before the manager's performance fee kicks in. Many private equity deals, for example, will state that the investor must first receive a 6% or 8% return on investment before the manager starts to take his 20% of the remaining profits. In a private equity context, this same idea is called a "preferred return."

IDRs, INCENTIVE DISTRIBUTION RIGHTS: These are essentially bonus income that gets paid to the managers of the MLP once the distributions to the LPs from the MLP hit a certain level. So the dollars might go something like: first $2 to investors, then, of the next $2, $1.75 to the LPs and 25 cents to the GPs; then, of the next dollar, fifty-fifty.

The traditional argument is that this just aligns the interests and the managers, so the greater the income the more they make. But, of course, there are other things the MLP could do with that money, like build the business. In many MLPs the IDRs are capped, or nonexistent. Note that often the worst deals for the MLP investors occur when the GPs are themselves traded entities, because then the GPs have their own, separate shareholders to worry about, setting up a conflict between the two sets of public investors.

ILLIQUIDITY PREMIUM: The extra return an investor receives as compensation for holding less than fully liquid asset or security.

ILS, INSURANCE-LINKED SECURITIES: These refer to a range of products that distribute insurance-type risks into the capital markets. Cat bonds (see page 233) are among the most popular, but there are several others, including extreme mortality and longevity swaps, reserve securitization, life insurance settlement trading, and weather derivatives (see page 259).

IMPLIED VOLATILITY: Any option price has a few components. The most important is the price of the security you're getting the right to buy or sell (known as the "underlying"). Then, there's the time value of money paid for the option. But that leaves the most interesting piece, the price that people are paying for the volatility of the option, which is *implied* by deducting the other, known, pricing elements from the exiting market price.

Black-Scholes (see above) is the classic formula that solved the ancient puzzle about how to price options. The key insight there was how to price the *historic* volatility of the underlying security: the more volatile the performance has been, the more valuable an option to buy or sell it is. So Black-Scholes essentially tells us what an option "should" be priced at, at least from an academic point of view. If a trader sees an implied volatility that is "out of line" with Black-Scholes, there might be an opportunity for volatility arbitrage.

INDEX ARBITRAGE: A favorite tactic of high-frequency traders, the idea is to exploit minor differences between the price of an ETF and the cumulative total of the prices of the stocks it holds. When they get slightly out of line, traders can profit by buying the ETF and selling the exact underlying basket of stocks; or vice versa.

INFORMATION RATIO: Similar to the Sharpe ratio. The easiest way to understand the difference is to think of return in three buckets: risk-free return; beta return; and alpha. The Sharpe ratio strips out the risk-free return and compares the combination of alpha and beta returns to risk taken. The information ratio is a bit more precise: it strips out both risk-free and beta returns, and focuses just on how much risk was taken to achieve the alpha component of the return. A good information ratio is something north of .5, and higher is better.

IRR: Stands for internal rate of return. Consider a real estate deal. If you just take the final sale proceeds of the investment, minus expenses along the way, to get a total profit and divide that profit by the total amount invested, you have a total percentage return. But to analyze the investment properly, you need to consider the time the dollars were invested and calculate how much you made on them each year. An IRR calculation accounts for not only when the initial investment was made but also, for example, when subsequent capital-improvement dollars went in, when cash flows came back, and generates an annual percentage rate of return on dollars while they were invested.

ISDA: The International Swaps and Derivatives Association is the trade group of the participants in most of the over-the-counter derivatives markets. ISDA has helped standardize documentation and processes for the industry, and essentially all the financial institutions in the world belong to it. The ISDA Determinations Committee has been, since 2009, the group that actually decides whether, for example, defaults have occurred under a credit default swap. It has therefore become a powerful force in global finance although it is not regulated or overseen by any governmental agencies.

J CURVE: For alternative investors, the J curve describes the process of making ongoing cash investments in a private equity or venture fund (or deal) while waiting for investments to start returning dollars. On a graph, the resulting shape looks like a *J*.

For economists, the J curve describes what is thought to generally happen after a currency devaluation. Although in the long run exports will become more price competitive, in the short run trade deficits may be exacerbated because domestic demand for foreign goods will not change instantly. (See page 137.)

KURTOSIS: A way of talking about tail risk. In a normal distribution bell curve, events out on the ends—the tails—of the bell curve are the extreme outcomes. Excess kurtosis means that we're looking at a bell curve with fat tails—an enhanced possibility of events that are out on the extreme ends of the curve.

LATENCY ARBITRAGE: This is a common term in the world of high-frequency trading and very generally refers to the idea that firms don't all get the same information about publicly traded stocks at exactly the same moment in time . . . some get it sooner and some later, and the difference is known as latency. Some trading firms spend fortunes to ensure they get the data first, and then profit from it by "latency arbitrage."

Say a mutual fund is in the market to buy a large quantity of a given stock. It will have algorithms execute the trade slowly, breaking the order down into small pieces, to try to get the best price. The program will offer to buy whatever's out there at, say, $4.50 per share, and then move on to what's available at $4.51, etc.

An HFT shop can see that a mutual fund–buying algorithm is in the market, and essentially front-runs its purchases, buying up all the available shares at $4.50 an instant before that slow-footed buyer is able to execute on it. Frustrated, the purchasing algorithm moves on, and looks to buy shares at

$4.51. Now the HFT program sells all the stock it just nabbed at $4.50 to the buying algorithm it knew was there all along, making a risk-free penny a share. At the volumes and speeds these things operate, that adds up.

LIQUID ALTERNATIVES: These include all traded securities that offer nontraditional strategies and assets. They can be grouped into income products and "smart beta" products. Income products include MLPs, royalty trusts, and high-yield bond ETFS. "Smart beta" products include long/short, managed futures, and other approaches that feature active risk management through shorting, derivatives, and other alternative approaches. In general, these securities carry lower fees than their private placement cousins, are fully registered with the SEC, and can be traded on an exchange or redeemed on any business day.

LOCKUP: In hedge funds, this refers to the minimum time period for which an investor must initially keep his money in a fund. Typically, that's one year, often with quarterly redemptions available after that (but often the investor can only get a given percentage of his money out on any given redemption date). Also, watch out for the required notice periods; it's common to require a warning of at least thirty days prior to a redemption.

In the start-up world, a lockup is an agreement between a company that is going public and its underwriters that insiders won't sell shares into the market for some period after the IPO, usually six months.

LONG/SHORT: In the typical long/short strategy, a manager picks a pair of stocks and bets that one will outperform the other. He can buy the one he expects to do better, and short the other; in principle, the trade will generate profits regardless of the general direction of the market, provided that the favored stock does *relatively* better than the other (goes up more in a bull market; falls less in a bear market). (See pages 30–32.)

MANAGED FUTURES: Refers to investments in "futures" that are "managed" by a professional on an investor's behalf . . . the person doing the investing is called a commodity trading advisor, or CTA. Most CTAs are "trend followers": they engage in programmatic trading based on the idea that once a price trend is in place, it will continue for a period of time. The strategies have generally provided results quite uncorrelated to the general financial markets. (See pages 48–50.)

MARKET NEUTRAL: A hedge strategy that is, in principle, completely indifferent to a market risk, usually meaning stock prices.

MERGER ARBITRAGE: In a typical merger, one company is effectively buying the stock of the other at a given price. After the merger is announced, but before it is consummated, the stock of the target typically hovers somewhere below the price that was offered, mostly because of the risks that the deal might not go through. To capitalize, a merger arbitrage manager can buy the target's stock while selling the acquirer's stock, capturing that price spread . . . if, of course, the deal goes through.

MEZZ: Short for "mezzanine," as in a theater. These securities are not on the top, nor on the bottom, of the capital stack: they sit between common equity and secured debt in terms of repayment rights. Mezz debt is particularly important in many LBO and real estate transactions, and many private equity firms specialize in making these kinds of high-yield loans.

MLPs: These are master limited partnerships, entities that are traded on public exchanges but not taxed at the entity level even though they conduct active businesses. Typically they hold infrastructure assets related to energy production and transportation, although other kinds exist. They often pay strong, tax-advantaged yields. (See pages 79–82.)

MODERN PORTFOLIO THEORY: A group of finance theories that seek to maximize the return on a portfolio for the cumulative risk taken by investing in that basket of securities. MPT depends on several ideas, including the efficient market hypothesis and that financial returns are "normally distributed," which are doubted by many.

NET EXPOSURE: This is a critical element in evaluating long/ short managers. Most do not run truly market neutral books and have a "bias" at any particular time. Perhaps they think that the market is headed up, so their positions may be 80% long and only 20% short. That would give the fund a "net long exposure" of 60%: 80 minus 20.

If the fund uses leverage (most do), it might have a "gross exposure" of more than 100%: it might be 120% long and 60% short, and so have a gross exposure of 180% but the same 60% net long exposure. (See page 104.)

NORMAL DISTRIBUTION: A pattern of probable outcomes that is traditionally visualized as the classic bell curve, on page 123. (See "reversion to the mean," below.)

NOTIONAL AMOUNT: In a derivates contract this is the reference amount against which interest and other payments are calculated. Take an interest rate swap as an example. In one of those, one party is paying a fixed rate, say 6%, and the other is paying floating, maybe LIBOR plus 2%. But those amounts have to be computed against some reference number. Let's say that's $1 million, so the fixed obligor is paying $60,000, and the floating might be paying $40,000. The notional—the reference amount—is $1,000,000; but the actual amounts at risk are much less.

OVERLAY: In the hedge fund world, overlay describes layering one trade or trading strategy on top of another in order to put a different risk or return twist on the underlying strategy. Imagine a manager who is long U.S. private equity and likes his positions, but he is very worried about the U.S. dollar risk. So he may stick with the PE portfolio but add a currency overlay by buying, for example, a bunch of Swiss franc ETFs.

PEER-TO-PEER: Direct lending (or other sort of investment transaction) between individuals or entities without the typical intermediation by banks or other financial institutions, typically facilitated through online portals.

PIK BONDS: Means "pay in kind," and these bonds permit the issuer to pay interest either in additional securities (more debt obligations) or in cash. Many have a feature called a "toggle"— the issuer can, whenever it wishes, start issuing more bonds in lieu of cash interest payments, but the "toggle notes" typically carry a higher coupon than the original bond.

PRE- AND POST-MONEY: These refer to the valuation of a private company before an investment is made, on the one hand, and after it's made, on the other.

The best way to think about these terms is to figure out what percentage the investor will get for his investment, and do the math to get to the postinvestment valuation; and then subtract the cash investment to get to the pre-money valuation. For example, let's say I have a start-up and I need $2 million to get through the next year. You say, OK, fine, I'll give you $2 million for 33% of the company. So immediately after the deal, you'll own one-third of the company for your investment. Thus, the post-money valuation is $6 million. The pre-money valuation would therefore be $4 million: the post-money valuation minus the actual dollars invested.

PREEMPTIVE RIGHTS: Preemptive rights give holders the future right, but not the obligation, to purchase shares from a company in sufficient quantities to maintain the holder's relative percentage ownership in the company in the event it issues new stock down the road. They are a kind of "antidilution" right.

Not all dilution is bad: if the subsequent rounds are at a big premium to the valuation you invested at, it might be fine. But if there's a down round, or if the subsequent investor comes in with preferred liquidation rights, or if—as will often be true in crowdfunded deals—the company "issues stock like confetti" . . . you'll want to have "preemptive rights."

PREFERRED RETURN: See "hurdle rate."

PRIVATE EQUITY FUND: A private partnership, pursuing longer term strategies, that invests in nontraded securities, and most often takes large ownership positions in private companies. The signature strategy is the "leveraged buyout," in which a fund borrows the maximum amount possible, and invests its own equity, to perform a corporate fixer-upper. Some PE firms also invest in specific infrastructure projects, growth stage private companies, roll-ups, and even other firms' buyouts ("mezz funds"). Broadly used, the term covers early-stage venture capital and real estate developments as well.

PRIVATE PLACEMENTS: Nonpublic securities are sold in "private placements," which can be bought only by accredited investors. Prior to the JOBS Act, private placements were even more private: they could not be advertised. But just because you can buy doesn't mean you can sell: numerous restrictions apply regarding to whom and how the securities can be resold, and typically investors in private placements liquidate their holdings by redemption instead of sale.

QUALIFIED CLIENT: Investment managers may charge incentive fees only to "qualified clients," which are individuals with a net worth of $2 million and institutions with assets over $5 million. Thus, the "20" in the famous "2 and 20" fee structure may be charged to fund investors only if they meet this standard.

RATCHET: A ratchet is an antidilution provision that makes sure that early investors will not lose a disproportionate share of their investment if subsequent investors come in.

Say a VC invests in a company through a preferred stock that converts into common at a valuation that equates to $1 per share. A "full ratchet" provision would say: if you subsequently sell common stock at less than $1, my conversion price will adjust downward, to whatever that lower price is. Something called a "weighted average ratchet" is more common (and more fair); this includes a formula that adjusts the ratchet in a way that keeps the initial investor's dilution minimal but doesn't overcompensate him in a down round.

REITs: Real estate investment trusts, the extremely popular way for the public to invest in the asset class, have the huge benefit of not being subject to tax at the entity level. But the price for that is that they must remain passive investors, holding assets and collecting lease and mortgage payments. (See page 96.)

REOCs: These are real estate operating companies, the opposite of REITs. They do actively operate real estate businesses, but they are taxable at the entity level.

REPO: The term is short for "repurchase," and it describes a deal in which one party sells a security for cash, but at the same time gets a contract to repurchase, or repo, it from the buyer at a higher price on a specific date. The difference in the purchase and sale prices is essentially an interest charge. Therefore, a repo is essentially a super-collateralized loan. The Fed uses repos and reverse repos to inject and withdraw liquidity into and from the banking system.

REVERSION TO THE MEAN: Think of individual waves hitting the beach. We know that as high tide arrives the average wave will gradually creep farther onto the sand. That average is very predictable, but the very next wave's reach onto the sand isn't. Even as the tide comes in, some waves will not come nearly as close to your chair as the previous ones did. But then most will come much closer. There is a "normal distribution" to the pattern of the waves . . . some closer, some not so close, but the average is predictable.

If several waves come up well short of your chair, a bunch of the next ones will come in much closer, or maybe go right by you. Those stronger waves are causing the average to "revert to the mean" as the tide comes in. You can bet on it happening. And traders do, all the time, in an enormous range of financial instruments.

RISK-ADJUSTED RETURNS: Financial results adjusted for the risks taken to achieve them. The biggest mistake most investors make is failing to consider this issue when evaluating managers, and instead chasing those with the biggest, latest, gross returns. The law of averages wins out over time.

RISK PREMIUMS: Ever since the crash, there has been an ongoing reevaluation of allocation strategies, and this is one of the big topics. Instead of thinking specifically about asset classes per se, allocators are looking at where they'll get paid the most for investing. A big source of income—maybe the biggest for most people—is the equity risk premium. Another big one is illiquidity. The fear level right now is so high that everyone is demanding liquidity in their investments. Others include size, enterprise, credit, interest rate, currency, and sovereign risks.

ROYALTY INTERESTS: The owner of a royalty pays a fixed amount for it and has a right to receive a stream of income generated by the underlying property, whether that's an energy field, a song, or a drug patent. Unlike a "working interest" holder of a drilling operation, for example, there is no obligation to continue funding the project. Royalties are a key alternative income source, and can be found in various packages, from royalty trusts to MLPs to many kinds of private placements.

R SQUARED: This is another key statistic for measuring investment managers. It illustrates how much of the portfolio's performance is explained by the overall movements of the market. It is measured on a scale of 1 to 100, with 100 meaning that all of the movement in the portfolio is explained by movement in the index. On the other hand, an R squared below 70 or so shows that the index and the portfolio are acting fairly differently from the overall market.

SHARPE RATIO: Financial returns divided by the relative volatility of the portfolio: the greater the volatility (equal to risk, in MPT terms), the lower the Sharpe. This number should appear in the marketing materials of the investment under consideration. Normally, a Sharpe of more than 1 is good, and more than 2 very good. (See pages 209–11.)

SIDE POCKET: Most often, hedge funds hold liquid assets. But sometimes funds do have illiquid assets, either by agreement with investors or because assets that were thought to be liquid turn out not to be. These are often held in a "side pocket" of the fund until they can be sold.

SIGMA: Refers to the standard deviation, or volatility, of a fund. Standard deviation is a measure of how well clustered a data set is around its mean. If most of the numbers in a series— say, monthly investment returns—are close to the average of those numbers, the standard deviation is low. But if there's a very wide band into which those results fall, if the numbers are widely dispersed as compared to the average, the standard deviation is high. So sigma indicates how erratic the returns have been. The higher the sigma, the greater the variation in the returns over time has been. In theory, that means more risk was taken.

SKEW OR SKEWNESS: Recall that most of the statistics used in analyzing investment performance depend on one key idea: that outcomes are normally distributed, as represented in that symmetrical bell curve on page 123. But in the real world many investments don't actually generate results that are so evenly distributed. There might be many more data points on one side of the mean than the other. That's skewness: negative skew if more data points are on the left, positive skew if they're on the right.

SMART BETA: Stock market exposure through active risk management strategies, usually in freely tradable or redeemable securities like mutual funds. They provide downside protection and upside participation with liquidity and low fees in a fully registered investment product. But what they won't typically provide is alpha.

SOFT DOLLARS: Refers to a kind of frequent-flier program that brokers offer to money managers. In exchange for business, brokers often provide benefits (like research) back to the money manager without cash compensation. Of course the reason is that they're making great money on the brokerage commissions and want to keep the manager as a client. So the expression is that those benefits are "soft dollared" back to the money manager. The opposite is that the money manager pays cash for the benefits, which are called "hard dollars."

SORTINO RATIO: A variation of the Sharpe ratio that distinguishes between "good volatility" (upside) and "bad volatility" (downside). Since most investors don't mind a manager whose extra volatility typically generates profits, it's a useful tool. (See pages 209–11.)

STAT ARB: Statistical arbitrage is a category of trading that usually involves massive, short-term trading of baskets of securities as to which the trader (usually an algorithm) detects a small pricing anomaly, and expects to see mean reversion or reestablishment of a historical relationship.

STRATEGIC ASSET ALLOCATION (SAA): See "endowment model."

STRUCTURED CREDIT: Refers to methods of slicing and dicing the risks and/or cash flows associated with a debt obligation, and transferring them out to different parties. The first generation of structured credit deals involved the pooling of loans. So instead of selling one mortgage to one buyer, a bank would throw a bunch of mortgages into a trust, and then sell off rights to receive cash flows from the whole trust to different buyers: first cash flows to Tranche A, second set of cash flows to B, etc. In this way nobody was assuming all the risks of a given mortgage. The structure changed how credit risks of the underlying loans were allocated, and hence the name. That kind of pooling led to an explosion of CMOs, CLOs, CDOs, etc., and most recently to credit default swap.

SUBORDINATION: A legal term that refers to rights as between different classes of claimants. The junior claimants, say noteholders, are said to be "subordinated" to senior secured bondholders. The senior guys get paid first, the junior guys are subordinated.

The most basic corporate law point of all is that equity holders are subordinated to bondholders in a corporate liquidation. But it's also extremely important in all distressed debt investing, structured credit instruments, CMOs and CDOs, etc. In all these, the biggest issues will revolve around who gets paid first, second, third. Who is subordinated to whom?

SWAPTION: As it sounds, a swaption is a combination of an option and a swap. Or, more specifically, the right, but not the obligation, to enter into a swap at some point in the future. Usually the underlying swap is an interest rate swap, so upon exercise one side would pay fixed and receive floating, and the other side would do the opposite.

SWFs: Sovereign wealth funds are sponsored by countries that have excess liquid assets, usually out of foreign exchange reserves. As you can guess, the first SWFs were from oil exporting countries like Saudi Arabia and Norway; more recently, Asian countries, like China, Singapore, and South Korea, have established them.

SWFs currently have about $5 trillion under management, growing about 10% per year. ADIA, the Abu Dhabi Investment Authority, is the single biggest fund, over $600 billion. But China has a few funds, totaling over $1.3 trillion, so it is actually the largest sovereign sponsor.

TED SPREAD: The difference between three-month LIBOR and U.S. T-bills. It's always been thought of as a critical measure of the health of the credit markets and the overall economy. In fact, the Fed itself has often used the TED spread as a factor in how things are going, whether they need to add liquidity to the system, change rates, etc.

About a half point spread is normal. When it gets to over 1, you've got some issues in the economy; over 2, it's looking bad. During the crisis, it jumped to over four.

TIMOs, TIMBERLAND INVESTMENT MANAGEMENT ORGANIZA-TIONS: Registered investment advisors for timberland. They don't own the land . . . instead they operate separately managed accounts for large institutional investors, like pension plans. TIMOs often have different specialties: hardwood forests, yield enhancement, different geographies, and so on.

TIPS, TREASURY INFLATION-PROTECTED SECURITIES: U.S. government debt obligations, the principal of which adjusts upward and downward (but, crucially, not below the face amount) as CPI fluctuates. (See pages 176–78.)

TOTAL RETURN SWAP: In a "total return swap," you're really buying a position from me, say a $1 million Spanish government bond. So I pay you the interest I receive on the reference asset, plus any appreciation I may get on it. You usually pay me something like LIBOR and a spread, but also the depreciation on the bond. This transfers both credit and market risk on the asset to you. Here, the notional amount probably won't turn into an obligation, but it could. If Spain blows up and defaults, you owe me the notional amount.

TREITS: A TREIT is a timber REIT, and, unlike a TIMO, it does own the land and the timber. Like normal REITs, these don't pay tax at the entity level and are listed securities, so they can be a good way for individual investors to get exposure to the asset class.

UCIT: A collective investment company organized under a set of rules that is increasingly popular around the world—outside the United States. They feature pretty strong governance requirements, independent custody, frequent but not daily liquidity, limited leverage, and reporting.

UNCORRELATED: Financial assets that perform differently from the stock and bond markets and, in a very well diversified portfolio, from each other as well. An uncorrelated portfolio will contain "divergent" strategies that perform better in periods of high volatility than do more traditional "convergent" strategies.

VAR: Meaning "value at risk," this is the maximum amount (in principle!) that a fund, strategy, or entity can lose in a given day; it's a crucial concept in overall risk management, and often determined by complex computer programs. Nearly all significant funds and financial institutions rely heavily on their "VAR models."

WATERFALL: Usually PE and VC fund managers receive a 2% management fee and an incentive fee of 20% of the upside. The question is how do the profits "flow" for purposes of making this calculation. There are two major varieties of waterfalls, European and American.

PE and venture funds make a series of investments at different times, and then dispose of them at different times. In a "European" waterfall, investors get all their invested capital back, plus a preferred return on all that capital, before the manager takes his fee. In an "American" fund, profits to the managers are calculated on a deal-by-deal basis instead, as each position of the fund is exited.

WEATHER DERIVATIVES: These are contracts that pay off if certain defined weather conditions exist, usually over a period of time. Firms can hedge out too many cold days this winter, too many hot ones in the summer, too much frost in the fall and rain in the spring. The originals were all unique and traded over the counter, but many are now traded and cleared through exchanges.

For example, derivatives for hot days work off an index for so-called CDDs, cooling degree days. The idea is to capture the number of days that require air-conditioning during a specific period, determined by how many of them exceed a temperature of, say, seventy-five degrees. The basic contract then pays x dollars for every CDD over the base number. (Also see "cat bonds.")

WORKING INTEREST: A type of ownership in an oil and gas lease. Owners of working interests are responsible for the costs of exploration, drilling, and production of the property, and they typically receive the lion's share of profits as a result. Compare these with "royalty interests."

Resources

General

Altanswer.com

The Web site for this book, with video explanations of most of the glossary terms, a constantly updated resources section, industry news, and lots of other bonus features. Please check it out!

www.altanswer.com

Rule501.com

Invite-only educational resource center for accredited investors, with access to selected private placements. You can request an invitation from the Altanswer Web site.

www.rule501.com

Opalesque

A top news and information resource for alternative investing providing daily newsletters and expansive text and video coverage of a wide range of strategies and managers.

www.opalesque.com

The Common Fund

The Common Fund is the leading investment firm servicing the nonprofit and pension investment communities. The Web site provides numerous excellent white papers and newsletters.

www.commonfund.org

BlackRock

A leader in investment management, risk management, and advisory services for institutional and retail clients worldwide; its Investment Institute procures well-respected insights on various markets and asset classes.

www.blackrock.com

Cambridge Associates
Global investment advisor with focus on foundations and endowments, family offices, institution investors, and private equity managers. Excellent source of research materials.
www.cambridgeassociates.com

Preqin
Another top-tier research provider. Preqin covers PE, VC, real estate, HFs, and infrastructure funds, and offers free access to indices.
www.preqin.com

Pertrac
Provides analytics, reporting, and communications software for investment professionals, with proprietary research and insights to the alternative investment universe. .
www.pertrac.com

Bloomberg
The one-stop shop for essential news and data for all things finance and money related.
www.bloomberg.com

Money Moves
Deirdre Bolton's Bloomberg Television show focused on alternative investing. Available on air and online around the world.
www.bloomberg.com/tv/shows/money-moves

The Alliance of Alternative Asset Professionals
TAAAPs is a nonprofit industry organization that provides educational materials for professionals and investors working in the alternative asset industry.
www.taaaps.org

Investment Platforms

Rule 501
(see page 261)
Invite-only resource center for accredited investors, with access to investment opportunities.
www.rule501.com

Gust
Platform specializing in start-up funding and angel investors. The Gust blog regularly features commentary from top players in the angel investing space.
www.gust.com

AngelList
Popular, "social proof" platform for connecting start-ups, investors, and talent.
https://angel.co

SecondMarket
SecondMarket is a type of stock market for many types of private issuers, allowing them to manage secondary liquidity, raise capital, and communicate with stakeholders.
www.secondmarket.com

CAIS-X
Platform that provides wealth managers with access to a range of investment opportunities, with special focus in alternatives.
www.caisgroup.com

Guggenheim Partners
Top-tier investment manager with an "alternatives platform" focused on hedge fund investing. Produces well-regarded market research and analysis.
www.guggenheimpartners.com

AxialMarket
Platform connecting private companies with 8,500+ accredited members.
www.axialmarket.com

Prosper.com
The largest peer-to-peer lending platform.
www.prosper.com

Lending Club
Another "P2P" site.
www.lendingclub.com

AlphaMetrix
AlphaMetrix Global Marketplace: secure software platform that integrates

portfolio, general ledger, and investor accounting with "Point-Click-Invest" capability. Provides real-time data and highly customizable user interfaces.
www.alphametrix.com

Hedge Fund Info

Alternative Investment Management Association (AIMA)
Excellent resource center for alternatives industry, with key practice guides and forms, as well as a quarterly journal and road map to hedge funds.
www.aima.org

The Hedge Fund Association
The HFA is a nonprofit trade and lobbying organization whose goal is to increase transparency and development in the alternative assets industry. Their Web site provides a useful compilation of pertinent industry publications, articles, and media.
www.thehfa.org

Preqin
(see page 262)
www.preqin.com

Opalesque
(see page 261)
www.opalesque.com

BarclayHedge
Alternative investments databases, with comprehensive data, reports, and information on the hedge fund, fund of funds, and CTAs space.
www.barclayhedge.com

Greenwich Alternative Investments
Greenwich Commercial Database: provides accredited individual investors with access to hedge fund and alternative investment data, research, statistics, search features, and hedge-fund index data.
www.greenwichai.com

CAIS-X
(see page 263)
www.caisgroup.com

Guggenheim Investments
Investment arm of Guggenheim Partners, with premier talent and data resources on hedge funds, ETFs, mutual funds, and other alternatives.
guggenheiminvestments.com

Private Equity General Info

Preqin
(see page 262)
www.preqin.com

Cambridge Associates
(see page 261)
www.cambridgeassociates.com

Private Equity and Growth Capital Council
Industry Web site that provides research, white papers, and presentations covering a range of topics including industry trends, tax considerations, and pertinent legislation. The PEGCC Web site contains two unique features that may prove especially useful to investors: case studies of successful PE investments and a state-by-state guide to private equity.
www.pegcc.org

AxialMarket
(see page 263)
www.axialmarket.com

Venture and Angel Info

Angel Capital Association
A professional group for North American angel investing groups and private investors, the ACA is an excellent resource for learning about angel investing, finding and joining angel groups, or networking with fellow investors. The ACA provides good basic education materials as well as interesting research papers and a useful newsletter covering the industry.
www.angelcapitalassociation.org

National Venture Capital Association
The NVCA is a professional organization for the venture capital industry that

provides data, statistics, and research to investors and VC firms alike. The NVCA has also created model legal documents, valuation guidelines, and an extensive library of educational materials.
www.nvca.org

Gust
(see page 261)
www.gust.com

AngelList
(see page 263)
https://angel.co

Y-Combinator
Innovative model for start-up funding, especially in digital and tech space. Its blog is a way to keep up-to-date on new, innovative companies, recent fund-raising, and acquisitions.
www.ycombinator.com

Kleiner Perkins Caufield & Byers (KPCB)
The classic VC firm. Its Insights reports provide thorough treatment of market trends with solid global macro overlays.
www.kpcb.com

First Round Capital
Leading New York–based venture capitalists specializing in very early-stage investing. In the Library section of the Web site you can find articles on start-ups and venture capital, as well as explanations of what they are investing in and why.
www.firstround.com

Farmland Informaton

Farmers' National
Farm management company that specializes in land auction sales, farm management services, and all related landowner services. Provides some good, basic information regarding investing in farmland and farm management services.
www.farmersnational.com

Seedstock
Company with dedicated blog and news resource that promotes sustainable farming and agricultural start-ups, with some treatment of investing in farmland and agriculture sector.
www.seedstock.com

Ceres Partners
Investment manager for large portfolio of farms in the Midwest. Resource center provides good basic information regarding farmland investing.
www.cerespartners.com

Oil and Gas Partnership Information

Oil and Gas Investments Bulletin
News source for oil and gas industry investing, with a focus on publicly traded companies. Includes a frequently updated blog and a subscription-based newsletter.
www.oilandgas-investments.com

Coachman Energy
Investment manager focused on oil and gas opportunities in the Bakken Shale region.
www.coachmanenergy.com

Emerging Markets/Global Blue Chips Information

Jubak Picks
Investment blog run by Jim Jubak, noted financial analyst and stock-picker, with model portfolios focused on emerging market stock positions.
www.Jubakpicks.com

Oppenheimer Funds
Provides an extensive library of resources with market updates, news, commentary, educational materials, guides, tools, and calculators.
www.opco.com

Managed Futures Information

Altegris
Investment manager dealing with a range of alternatives, and specializing in managed futures. Produces many informative white papers focusing on market developments and the managed futures space.
www.altegris.com/en/Gateway.aspx

The Managed Funds Association
Its Web site provides extensive educational resources and timely industry and policy research.
www.managedfunds.org

Stark & Company
Research house that specializes in managed futures. Provides various CTA and managed future indices and CTA rankings.
www.starkresearch.com

Attain Capital Management
Specialized asset manager focused on both trading system and managed futures investments that provides a regularly updated managed futures blog.
www.managed-futures-blog.attaincapital.com

Gold Information

The London Bullion Market Association
Provides publicly accessible current and historical data on spot and forward gold prices, as well as industry research.
www.lbma.org.uk

Tocqueville Asset Management
Asset manager with expertise and solid track record investing and advising in gold-related funds and strategies. Produces regular newsletters about gold market and funds.
www.tocqueville.com

Royalty Information

Songvest.com
Venue for exchange of rights and royalties associated with music. Web site provides some basic information regarding music royalties.
www.songvest.com

The Royalty Exchange
Auction platform that provides a marketplace for the exchange of movie, book, television, patent, trademark, pharmaceutical, and music royalties. Maintains a blog that tends to focus on developments in entertainment-related royalties.
www.theroyaltyexchange.com

Master Limited Partnerships (MLPs) Information

Miller/Howard Investments, Inc.
Investment boutique with expertise in MLPs. Provides a fairly extensive and regularly updated library of white papers relating to MLPs and income-investing, as well as a quarterly report.
www.mhinvest.com

Center Coast
RIA focusing on energy-related MLPs, with an extensive database of research and publications on MLPs.
www.centercoastcap.com

SteelPath
Its research center provides good background information regarding MLPs, as well as regularly produced white papers and fund commentary.
www.steelpath.com/individual/research-education

Liquid Alternatives

Morningstar
Excellent research site for all liquid alternatives.
www.morningstar.com

iShares (by BlackRock)
Specializes in registered funds with both active and passive strategies through its iShares ETFs. Its Insights page offers market commentary and investment theses with an ETF slant, as well as numerous ETF-related white papers.
www.ishares.com

KKR
Leading global investment firm and advisor rooted in private equity.
www.kkr.com

Blackstone
Premier global investment and advisory firm specializing in alternative asset management; excellent resource for market commentary.
www.blackstone.com

Registered Privates

Registered Fund Services
Provides information and services regarding registered privates.
www.umbfs.com/RegisteredHedgeFunds

Family Offices

Institute for Private Investors
Peer networking site for private investors and family offices, providing thought leadership and education for similarly minded investors.
www.memberlink.net

Family Office Exchange (FOX)
World's largest peer-to-peer network and research database for ultra-wealthy families and their family offices.
www.familyoffice.com

About the Author

Bob Rice is Bloomberg TV's Alternative Investments Editor, the managing partner at Tangent Capital, and a board member of investment advisors with more than $2 billion under management. The positions he has held throughout his multifaceted career have spanned many domains: Wall Street law firm partner; public company CEO; trial lawyer for the U.S. Department of Justice; and technology entrepreneur.